ZERO TRUST
PLAYBOOK

*A Cybersecurity Strategy
Inspired by the Soccer Field*

Dr. Jerry Yonga

DEDICATION

To my family, who have been my steadfast support and inspiration through every challenge.

To my students, whose curiosity and passion remind me daily of the importance of sharing knowledge and the power of continuous learning.

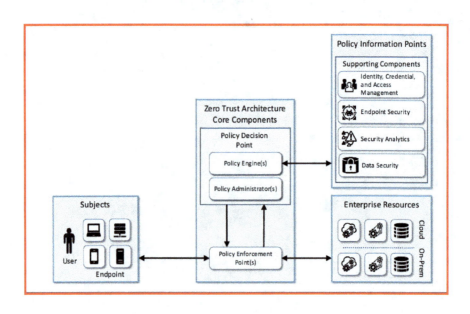

CONTENTS

ACKNOWLEDGMENTS

I am deeply grateful to the **National Institute of Standards and Technology (NIST)** for their invaluable contributions to the field of **Zero Trust Architecture**. Their work, particularly **Special Publication 800-207**, served as a key resource for this book.

I extend my thanks to my **colleagues, students, and cybersecurity professionals** whose insights and real-world experiences have enriched this project. Your shared knowledge has made this work more practical and grounded.

A heartfelt thanks to my **family** especially my grandkids (Danielle, Nicole, Remy, and Cosby) for their constant support and patience throughout the writing process. This book is a testament to your encouragement and belief in my vision.

— **Prof. Jerry Yonga**

A New Era of Cybersecurity—Trust No One, Verify Everything

In the world of cybersecurity, there was a time when digital fortresses held the line. Strong walls—firewalls—were built to keep intruders out and valuable data safe within. This traditional approach to cybersecurity thrived on the belief that if you could control what entered your network, you could protect everything inside. But as digital landscapes evolved, this strategy began to show its cracks. The walls could not keep pace with the expanding footprint of cloud computing, remote work, and interconnected devices. And in 2015, a seismic event changed everything: the **Office of Personnel Management (OPM) data breach,** exposing the sensitive records of over **22 million people.**

This breach, one of the largest in U.S. history, was a wake-up call that highlighted the vulnerabilities of traditional network defenses. Attackers slipped past the perimeter using stolen credentials, then moved freely within the network—unnoticed—like players running unchecked across a soccer field. This lateral movement, where attackers

1

escalate privileges and access more sensitive information from within, revealed a glaring flaw in the old way of thinking: **inside the network was never truly safe**.

From this critical realization, a new philosophy emerged—**Zero Trust**. The essence of Zero Trust is simple yet radical: **"Never Trust, Always Verify."** It acknowledges that breaches are inevitable and that the perimeter has dissolved. Instead of assuming anything is safe, Zero Trust starts with the idea that **every access request—whether from inside or outside—must be verified, scrutinized, and authenticated** before allowing access to resources.

The traditional security approach is like playing a soccer match believing the opponents are always outside the field. But what if some of them were already on the inside, disguised as teammates? Zero Trust changes the game by assuming every player, whether inside or outside, needs to prove their legitimacy constantly. It is not about building a bigger fence; it's about scrutinizing every move, every pass, every goal attempt. This shift from building perimeters to enforcing continuous verification creates a security environment where **trust is not granted by location but earned through constant validation**.

As the **National Institute of Standards and Technology (NIST)** began exploring Zero Trust principles, it became clear that this new model required not just a technological shift but a change in mindset— a transformation of how organizations think about security. In **2018**, the NIST **National Cybersecurity Center of Excellence (NCCoE)** launched a project to bring these concepts to life, guiding federal agencies and the broader industry toward a more resilient and adaptive security architecture. By **2020**, the **NIST Special Publication 800-207** provided a blueprint for adopting Zero Trust, laying out the principles, deployment models, and use cases that would guide organizations through this transition.

This book aims to demystify Zero Trust using an analogy from the soccer field—where technical skills, tactical strategies, physical strength, and psychological resilience all play a role in shaping a winning game. In the same way, **technical tools**, **strategic approaches**, **physical security measures**, and **leadership mindsets** shape a successful Zero Trust strategy. Just as in soccer, where players must constantly adapt to opponents' moves, a Zero Trust approach requires organizations to adapt to evolving cyber threats, ensuring that access is **continuously monitored** and **never taken for granted**.

Zero Trust is more than a set of rules or technologies—it is a new way of thinking about security in a world where the threats are no longer at the gates; they are already inside. The journey through this book will explore the **technical foundations**, **tactical approaches**, **physical safeguards**, and the **psychological shifts** needed to embrace Zero Trust, turning every organization into a resilient defender on the cybersecurity field. The time to trust no one and verify everything has come.

Welcome to the world of Zero Trust. Let's step onto the field and start the game.

1 Introduction to Zero Trust Architecture: A Comprehensive Approach

- Understanding the Need for Zero Trust
- A Brief History of Cybersecurity and the Evolution to Zero Trust
- Overview of the Soccer Analogy in Cybersecurity

Understanding the Need for Zero Trust

The landscape of cybersecurity has evolved significantly over the past decade, driven by the increasing complexities of **cloud computing**, **remote work**, and **mobile device usage**. Traditional security models once relied on **perimeter defenses**—like firewalls—that treated the network as a secure enclave. This approach is often likened to a medieval castle: build robust walls to keep out intruders, and everything inside is trusted implicitly. However, as the digital landscape expanded, the flaws in this method became increasingly apparent.

A pivotal event highlighting these weaknesses was the **Office of Personnel Management (OPM) data breach in 2015.** Attackers leveraged stolen credentials to access internal systems, moving laterally and undetected to extract sensitive information on over **22 million individuals**. This breach underscored a critical issue: once attackers were inside the network, they could operate freely, exploiting the **implicit trust** that traditional security models granted to internal traffic. This kind of movement, where threats navigate within the network rather than breaching from the outside, is often referred to as **East-West traffic**.

In response to these vulnerabilities, the concept of **Zero Trust** emerged. Zero Trust operates on a simple yet transformative principle: **"Never Trust, Always Verify."** This means that **every access request** to resources, regardless of origin—inside or outside the network—must be authenticated, authorized, and subject to continuous monitoring. Unlike older models that presumed trust based on location, Zero Trust assumes that **breaches are inevitable**. Therefore, it mandates continuous verification of user identities, device health, and the context of each request.

The formalization of this approach came with the **NIST Special Publication 800-207,** which provides a framework for implementing Zero Trust. This guide emphasizes the need to move beyond network perimeters and focus on **resource-centric security**, where each **user, device, and application** is treated as a potential threat until proven otherwise. It recognizes that, in a world of cloud-based services and distributed workforces, the network perimeter can no longer serve as a reliable boundary for trust.

Zero Trust also emphasizes **minimizing attack surfaces** through strategies like **micro-segmentation**—dividing the network into isolated zones to limit how far an attacker can move if they do gain access. This segmentation is akin to creating tightly controlled zones on a soccer field, where defenders monitor every move and contain potential threats before they can cause damage.

A Brief History of Cybersecurity and the Evolution to Zero Trust

The journey from **perimeter-based defenses** to **Zero Trust** marks a significant shift in cybersecurity philosophy. In the early days, tools like **firewalls** and **Virtual Private Networks (VPNs)** were considered the backbone of network security. These tools assumed that threats came from outside the network and that internal activities could be trusted. This assumption worked well when networks were simpler and less interconnected, but as **cloud services** and **remote access** became more common, it became a liability.

Incidents like the **OPM data breach**, as well as high-profile breaches at **Equifax** and **Yahoo**, highlighted how attackers could bypass external defenses and exploit internal vulnerabilities. Once attackers gained initial access, they could navigate the internal systems without detection, leveraging **trust-based permissions** to reach sensitive data.

As breaches grew more sophisticated, organizations recognized the need for **continuous monitoring** and **granular access control**. This realization led to the development of **Zero Trust Architecture (ZTA)** in the **mid-2010s,** a shift supported by organizations like the **NIST National Cybersecurity Center of Excellence (NCCoE).** In **2020,** NIST released its **Special Publication 800-207,** which provided a blueprint for adopting Zero Trust principles across industries. This document emphasized key concepts like:

- **Continuous Authentication**: Requiring users and devices to re-verify their identity each time they request access to a resource, rather than trusting them after an initial login.
- **Least Privilege Access**: Granting users the minimum access necessary for their role, reducing the potential damage from compromised accounts.
- **Real-Time Analytics**: Using **threat intelligence** and **behavior analytics** to adjust access policies dynamically, ensuring that the security posture adapts as threats evolve.

These principles transformed the approach to cybersecurity, focusing on securing **individual resources** rather than defending a broad perimeter.

Overview of the Soccer Analogy in Cybersecurity

To grasp how Zero Trust functions, it is helpful to draw a parallel with **soccer,** where the balance between offense and defense is key to success. In soccer, players must remain vigilant throughout the game, adapting their tactics as the opposing team shifts its strategy. Similarly, Zero Trust requires **continuous adaptation** and **dynamic responses** to potential threats, ensuring that no part of the network is left unprotected.

- **Technical Skills (The Tools of Defense)**: In soccer, technical skills like passing, shooting, and defending are fundamental. In a Zero Trust environment, these skills correspond to **technical tools** such as **Endpoint Detection and Response (EDR)**, **firewalls**, and **encryption**. These tools form the frontline defense, monitoring for anomalies and responding swiftly to suspicious activities.

- **Tactical Approaches (Strategic Defense)**: Just as soccer coaches devise strategies to counter different opponents, cybersecurity professionals use **tactical planning** in Zero Trust. This includes **penetration testing, deception techniques** like **honeypots**, and **adaptive access controls**. These strategies help anticipate attacks and adjust security measures to stay ahead of evolving threats.

- **Physical Strength (Infrastructure and Devices)**: In soccer, a team's physical stamina is essential for maintaining performance. In cybersecurity, this translates to the **physical infrastructure** that supports Zero Trust, including **secure data centers, network appliances**, and **hardware firewalls**. These components ensure that the core network remains resilient against both physical and digital threats.

- **Psychological Resilience (Leadership and Culture)**: Soccer players rely on a strong mindset to perform under pressure. Similarly, a **Zero Trust strategy** relies on **leadership decisions, organizational culture**, and the commitment to

8

continuous improvement. This involves adopting policies that prioritize **security awareness** and maintaining a **mindset of vigilance**, where no access is taken for granted.

By viewing Zero Trust through this soccer analogy, it becomes clear that a successful Zero Trust strategy is not just about deploying technical tools; it involves coordination, strategy, and a commitment to continuous verification. Just as a soccer team adjusts its tactics throughout a match, organizations must continually adapt their security posture to counter new threats.

Conclusion

This chapter lays the foundation for understanding the **core principles of Zero Trust Architecture** and the need for a shift from **perimeter-based security** to **resource-centric protection**. By exploring the **historical context, NIST's role in defining Zero Trust**, and the **soccer analogy**, readers gain a clear picture of how this approach addresses modern cybersecurity challenges. As we proceed, the following chapters will delve deeper into the **technical skills, tactical strategies, physical measures**, and **leadership mindsets** that shape an effective Zero Trust strategy, equipping organizations with the knowledge to defend their networks in an ever-changing threat landscape.

2 Technical Skills: The Building Blocks of Zero Trust

- Identity and Access Management (IAM): Guarding the Goal
- Encryption, VPNs, and Data Protection Strategies
- Endpoint Detection and Response (EDR): Monitoring Threats in Real-Time
- Firewalls and Intrusion Detection Systems (IDS): Defending the Perimeter
- Case Study: Implementing Technical Tools in Healthcare

Introduction

In the game of cybersecurity, **technical skills** are the core defensive tactics that form the basis of a robust **Zero Trust Architecture (ZTA)**. Much like the fundamental abilities required of soccer players—passing, dribbling, and shooting—the technical tools in Zero Trust are essential for defending against potential threats. They include systems for **identity verification, data protection, real-time threat detection,** and **perimeter defense**. In this chapter, we explore these critical building blocks, offering a detailed look into their roles, implementation, and importance in maintaining a secure digital environment.

Identity and Access Management (IAM): Guarding the Goal

In soccer, the goalkeeper's role is to guard the goal—no ball should get past them. Similarly, **Identity and Access Management (IAM)** is the gatekeeper of digital systems, ensuring that only **authorized users** gain access to sensitive resources. IAM systems verify **user identity** and determine what resources users are permitted to access based on their **roles** and **attributes**.

Key Concepts in IAM:

- **Authentication**: Verifying that users are who they claim to be using methods like **passwords, biometrics,** or **Multi-Factor Authentication (MFA)**.

- **Authorization**: Determining what actions users can perform once authenticated, often through **Role-Based Access Control (RBAC)** or **Attribute-Based Access Control (ABAC)**.

- **Single Sign-On (SSO)**: Allows users to authenticate once and gain access to multiple applications without having to log in again, streamlining user experience while maintaining security.

Importance in Zero Trust: In a Zero Trust environment, IAM is crucial for implementing **least privilege access**, meaning users only have access to what they absolutely need. This minimizes the risk of unauthorized access to sensitive data if credentials are compromised. NIST's Zero Trust guidelines emphasize the use of **dynamic and context-aware IAM policies**, where access is continuously re-evaluated based on **user behavior, location,** and **device posture**.

Encryption, VPNs, and Data Protection Strategies

In soccer, passing the ball requires precision to ensure it reaches the intended player. Similarly, **data encryption** ensures that sensitive information is securely transmitted between devices, protecting it from interception by unauthorized parties. **Virtual Private Networks (VPNs)** and other **data protection** strategies further ensure that data remains safe during transit and storage.

Key Concepts:

- **Encryption**: Converts data into a coded format that can only be deciphered with a decryption key, making it unreadable to unauthorized parties. It is used for both **data at rest** (stored data) and **data in transit** (data being transmitted).

- **VPNs**: VPNs create an **encrypted tunnel** for data to travel through, protecting it from eavesdropping on public networks. Although VPNs were once central to remote access, **Zero Trust Network Access (ZTNA)** is increasingly preferred as it provides more granular control over access.

- **Data Loss Prevention (DLP)**: Tools that monitor data flows to detect and prevent the **unauthorized transfer** of sensitive information, such as customer data or intellectual property.

Importance in Zero Trust: Encryption is a fundamental aspect of Zero Trust because it ensures that even if data is intercepted, it cannot be read without the encryption key. **NIST Special Publication 800-207** emphasizes the use of encryption and secure communication protocols as part of a **Zero Trust deployment**. By using VPNs or ZTNA, organizations can provide **secure remote access**, verifying user identity and device posture before allowing access to any data or applications.

Endpoint Detection and Response (EDR): Monitoring Threats in Real-Time

In soccer, defenders must constantly monitor the opposing team's movements, adjusting their positions to block potential attacks. **Endpoint Detection and Response (EDR)** plays a similar role in Zero Trust, monitoring **endpoint devices** such as laptops, servers, and mobile devices for **signs of suspicious activity**.

Key Concepts in EDR:

- **Real-Time Monitoring**: EDR agents installed on endpoints continuously collect data on processes, connections, and user actions, looking for anomalies.
- **Threat Hunting**: Analysts use EDR tools to proactively search for indicators of compromise (IoCs) or tactics used by attackers.
- **Automated Remediation**: When an EDR system detects a threat, it can automatically **isolate the affected device**, **terminate malicious processes**, or **quarantine files**.

Importance in Zero Trust: EDR is critical for **continuous visibility** across all devices in a Zero Trust environment. Since Zero Trust assumes that threats may already exist within the network, EDR tools are used to detect and mitigate these threats before they can spread. By integrating EDR data into **SIEM (Security Information and Event Management)** systems, organizations can gain a **holistic view of threats** across their entire IT infrastructure.

Firewalls and Intrusion Detection Systems (IDS): Defending the Perimeter

Even in a Zero Trust model, where every access is continuously verified, **firewalls** and **Intrusion Detection Systems (IDS)** remain crucial for protecting network boundaries, much like defensive lines in soccer that prevent attackers from approaching the goal.

Key Concepts:

- **Next-Generation Firewalls (NGFWs)**: Modern firewalls that offer capabilities beyond simple packet filtering, such as **application-layer inspection, deep packet inspection (DPI)**, and **intrusion prevention**.

- **Intrusion Detection Systems (IDS)**: Monitor network traffic for suspicious activities that could indicate an attack, such as unusual traffic patterns or attempts to access restricted areas of the network.

- **Intrusion Prevention Systems (IPS)**: An extension of IDS that can **automatically block detected threats** in real-time.

Importance in Zero Trust: While Zero Trust shifts focus away from traditional perimeter security, **defense-in-depth** strategies remain relevant. NGFWs and IDS help **segment networks** and **monitor ingress and egress traffic**, adding another layer of protection in case attackers bypass other security measures. NIST's Zero Trust framework suggests using firewalls in combination with **micro-segmentation** to limit **East-West traffic**, ensuring that even if one part of the network is compromised, access to other areas is restricted.

Case Study: Implementing Technical Tools in Healthcare

Healthcare organizations handle highly sensitive **patient data**, making them prime targets for cyberattacks. Implementing a Zero Trust model in such environments requires integrating **technical tools** to ensure **data privacy** and **regulatory compliance** under frameworks like **HIPAA**.

- **Challenge**: A hospital network managing patient records faced a growing number of **phishing attacks** and **ransomware threats** targeting endpoint devices used by medical staff.

- **Solution**: The hospital deployed **CrowdStrike EDR** across all devices, enabling real-time monitoring of medical workstations, tablets, and servers. They integrated EDR with their **SIEM system** to correlate threat data from endpoints with network logs, enhancing detection capabilities.

- **Outcome**: When a doctor's tablet was compromised through a phishing link, the EDR system automatically isolated the device, preventing the spread of **ransomware** to other parts of the network. Simultaneously, **IAM** controls ensured that unauthorized access to patient records was blocked, even from compromised accounts.

- **Lesson Learned**: Combining **technical defenses** like EDR, IAM, and NGFWs allows healthcare organizations to maintain **Zero Trust principles**, ensuring that **no single point of failure** can jeopardize patient data security.

Conclusion

Technical skills are the foundation of a robust Zero Trust strategy, enabling organizations to **control access**, **protect data**, and **detect**

threats in real-time. While traditional cybersecurity approaches focused on building barriers, Zero Trust requires a dynamic interplay between **identity management, data protection, endpoint visibility,** and **network segmentation**. By mastering these technical tools, organizations can ensure that every action is scrutinized, every device is monitored, and every access request is evaluated with a **"never trust, always verify"** mindset. As we move into the next chapters, we will explore how tactical strategies further enhance these technical defenses, making Zero Trust a complete game plan for modern cybersecurity.

.

3 Tactical Approaches: Strategy and Adaptation in Zero Trust

- Penetration Testing: Proactively Identifying Vulnerabilities
- Ethical Hacking and Red Team Exercises: Learning from the Offense
- Honeypots and Deception Technologies: Luring Attackers
- Adaptive Access Control and Single Sign-On (SSO)
- Case Study: Tactical Adaptations in Financial Services

Introduction

The implementation of **Zero Trust Architecture (ZTA)** goes beyond deploying technical tools; it requires a strategic mindset and tactical agility to adapt to evolving threats. Much like a soccer team that adjusts its formation and strategy based on the opponent's playstyle, organizations must leverage **tactical approaches** to proactively address vulnerabilities, anticipate threats, and adapt their defenses. This chapter explores key tactical strategies that support Zero Trust, including **penetration testing, ethical hacking, honeypots, adaptive access controls**, and **Single Sign-On (SSO)**. Real-life examples from industries such as **financial services** illustrate how these strategies can be applied to enhance organizational security.

Penetration Testing: Proactively Identifying Vulnerabilities

Penetration testing (pen testing) is the cybersecurity equivalent of a pre-season match where the team tests its strengths and weaknesses. Pen testers simulate attacks on an organization's systems to identify vulnerabilities before malicious actors can exploit them. These tests are essential in a Zero Trust framework, as they challenge the assumption that any part of the network is inherently secure.

Types of Penetration Testing:

- **External Pen Testing**: Targets systems and applications exposed to the internet, such as web servers, email gateways, and cloud-based services. This approach helps identify how external attackers might gain a foothold in the network.

- **Internal Pen Testing**: Simulates an insider threat, such as an employee with compromised credentials or a hacker who has already breached the perimeter. It focuses on **lateral movement**, testing whether attackers can access other systems from an initial entry point.

- **Web Application Pen Testing**: Examines web-based services for vulnerabilities like **SQL injection**, **cross-site scripting (XSS)**, and **authentication flaws**. This is particularly critical for organizations that rely heavily on web applications.

Real-Life Example: Equifax Data Breach (2017) In 2017, **Equifax** suffered a massive data breach due to an **unpatched vulnerability** in its **Apache Struts** web application. The breach exposed sensitive information of **147 million individuals**. Had Equifax conducted regular **web application penetration testing**, it could have identified the vulnerability and patched it before attackers exploited it. This example illustrates the importance of continuously testing and validating the security of web-facing applications to maintain a Zero Trust posture【95†source】.

Pen testing aligns with **NIST's Zero Trust principles** by helping organizations identify weaknesses in their **access control policies** and **segmentation strategies**【94†source】. By simulating real-world attack scenarios, pen tests provide a proactive defense against potential breaches, ensuring that even if attackers manage to gain access, their ability to move laterally is restricted.

Ethical Hacking and Red Team Exercises: Learning from the Offense

Ethical hacking and **Red Team exercises** go beyond identifying technical vulnerabilities by testing the **response capabilities** of an organization's security team. These exercises simulate sophisticated, **persistent attacks**, providing an opportunity for the **Blue Team** (defenders) to improve their detection and response skills.

Key Concepts:

- **Red Team:** A group that acts as **advanced adversaries**, using techniques similar to those employed by cybercriminals. Their goal is to find weaknesses that a typical pen test might miss, such as **social engineering vulnerabilities** or **gaps in incident response**.

- **Blue Team:** The internal security team responsible for **defending against attacks**. The Blue Team uses tools like **EDR** and **SIEM** systems to monitor network activity, detect threats, and respond to incidents.

- **Purple Team**: A collaborative approach where **Red and Blue Teams** work together to strengthen defenses. This ensures that insights from the Red Team's activities directly translate into improved detection and mitigation strategies for the Blue Team.

Real-Life Example: Microsoft's Red Team Operations Microsoft uses a dedicated Red Team to simulate attacks against its internal infrastructure. This team has identified potential weaknesses in **cloud security configurations,** which led to improvements in how **Azure security features** are deployed and monitored. The **Red Team's findings** directly inform **product updates** and **security policies,** helping Microsoft maintain a **Zero Trust environment** that continually adapts to emerging threats. This approach has enabled Microsoft to stay ahead of threats like **nation-state actors** targeting cloud services 【94†source】 【95†source】 .

In a Zero Trust framework, Red Team exercises are particularly valuable because they test the **effectiveness of adaptive access controls** and **response mechanisms**. According to **NIST Special Publication 800-207**, organizations should use Red Team insights to continuously refine their access control policies and ensure that threats are detected quickly, even if they originate from within the network 【94†source】 .

Honeypots and Deception Technologies: Luring Attackers
In the game of soccer, a player might use a feint to mislead their opponent into making a mistake. **Honeypots** and **deception technologies** perform a similar function in cybersecurity by setting traps for attackers, allowing security teams to study their behavior and

tactics.

Key Deception Techniques:

- **Honeypots**: Simulated systems that mimic real servers or databases, designed to attract attackers. Honeypots often appear to contain valuable information but are isolated from critical systems, allowing security teams to **monitor intrusions** without risking data loss.

- **Honeytokens**: Fake credentials, files, or **API keys** planted in systems or repositories. When attackers attempt to use these tokens, it alerts the organization to a possible breach.

- **Deception Grids**: Advanced systems that create a **virtual maze** of false data and systems, making it difficult for attackers to distinguish real assets from decoys. This technique not only slows down attackers but also increases the likelihood of **early detection**.

Real-Life Example: JPMorgan Chase's Deception Strategy

JPMorgan Chase implemented **honeypots** as part of its cybersecurity strategy to identify attackers targeting its **banking systems**. By deploying decoy servers that mimicked real financial databases, JPMorgan could monitor how attackers tried to exploit vulnerabilities and use this data to improve its **firewall rules** and **access controls**. This proactive approach allowed the bank to **fortify real systems** based on observed attack patterns, reducing the risk of successful breaches 【95†source】.

Deception technologies align with Zero Trust by providing **early warning systems** and insights into how attackers operate within a network. According to **NIST**, deception technologies can enhance

threat intelligence and help organizations adjust their **security policies** based on **real-time threat data**, creating a more adaptive security posture 【94†source】 .

Adaptive Access Control and Single Sign-On (SSO)

In soccer, a team adjusts its formation based on how the opponent plays. Similarly, **adaptive access control** dynamically adjusts access permissions based on **contextual factors**, ensuring that every access request is scrutinized for potential risks. **Single Sign-On (SSO)** simplifies access while ensuring that security policies are enforced uniformly across applications.

Key Concepts:

- **Adaptive Access Control**: Uses **contextual data** such as user behavior, device location, and **risk scores** to adjust access privileges. For example, if a user's device is flagged as compromised, adaptive controls can limit access to only essential applications until the issue is resolved.

- **Single Sign-On (SSO)**: Allows users to authenticate once and gain access to multiple applications. In a Zero Trust context, SSO is combined with **Multi-Factor Authentication (MFA)** to ensure that even if credentials are compromised, additional verification steps prevent unauthorized access.

- **Conditional Access Policies**: These policies define **rules for access** based on **real-time analysis**. For instance, access may be restricted during **unusual login times** or from **new locations** until further verification is completed.

Real-Life Example: Google's BeyondCorp Initiative Google

adopted a **Zero Trust model** through its **BeyondCorp** initiative, which eliminated traditional VPNs in favor of **adaptive access controls**. BeyondCorp uses **contextual data** to evaluate each user request, adjusting access based on factors like **device security** and **network location**. This approach allows Google to provide **seamless access** for its employees while maintaining tight control over who accesses its internal applications. By leveraging **SSO** integrated with **MFA**, Google ensures that access is **secure and efficient**, even for remote workers 【95†source】.

Adaptive access control supports the **Zero Trust principle** of **continuous verification**, as outlined in **NIST SP 800-207** 【94†source】. It ensures that access is always **context-aware**, reducing the risk of compromised credentials leading to unauthorized access.

Case Study: Tactical Adaptations in Financial Services
The financial services industry faces constant threats from cybercriminals seeking to exploit **customer data, transaction systems**, and **internal trading platforms**. To mitigate these risks, financial institutions have adopted **Zero Trust strategies** that emphasize **continuous testing** and **real-time adaptation**.

- **Challenge**: A major global bank experienced multiple attempts at **credential stuffing**, where attackers used previously stolen passwords to try to gain access to user accounts. The bank also faced internal threats, where compromised employee accounts were used to access sensitive customer data.

- **Solution**: The bank implemented a multi-layered Zero Trust approach that included:

- o **Red Team exercises** to simulate **credential stuffing attacks** and test the bank's detection capabilities.

- o **Adaptive access controls** that required **MFA** for high-risk activities, such as accessing customer data from new devices.

- o **Honeypots** deployed within trading platforms to identify unauthorized attempts to access trading algorithms and financial data.

- o **Web Application Penetration Testing** to regularly assess the security of their customer-facing platforms, identifying weaknesses in **API security** and **input validation**.

- **Outcome**: The combination of **adaptive access control** and **deception technologies** allowed the bank to detect unauthorized access attempts early, preventing attackers from moving laterally through the network. The **Red Team exercises** improved the responsiveness of the internal security team, reducing the time between detection and containment of potential breaches. This approach not only protected customer data but also ensured compliance with industry regulations like **PCI DSS** (Payment Card Industry Data Security Standard).

This case study illustrates how **tactical adaptations**—from **pen testing** and **ethical hacking** to **deception techniques**—help financial institutions maintain a **Zero Trust posture** in the face of constantly evolving threats. It demonstrates the importance of **real-time adjustments** and **proactive testing** in building a resilient security framework.

Conclusion

Tactical approaches are critical in achieving the **dynamic adaptability** required for an effective Zero Trust Architecture. Techniques like **penetration testing**, **Red Team exercises**, **honeypots**, and **adaptive access control** provide the **proactive defense** necessary to identify and respond to threats before they can cause significant damage. By continuously testing their defenses and adapting to new threats, organizations can ensure that their Zero Trust strategies remain **robust and relevant**.

The real-life examples in this chapter underscore the value of **learning from the offense** to strengthen defense, demonstrating that a successful Zero Trust strategy involves more than deploying tools—it requires **strategic foresight**, **collaborative effort**, and **constant vigilance**. As we move forward in the book, these concepts will be further applied to **specific industry contexts** and **technical implementations**, offering a deeper understanding of how to build a **resilient Zero Trust environment**.

4 Physical Security: Infrastructure That Supports Zero Trust

- Securing Data Centers and Servers
- Hardware Firewalls, Network Appliances, and IoT Devices
- Biometric Authentication: Building Secure Physical Access Points
- Managing Secure Wi-Fi and Physical Network Connections
- Case Study: Physical Security and Zero Trust in Manufacturing

Introduction

While much of **Zero Trust Architecture (ZTA)** focuses on securing digital pathways and access points, a critical and often underappreciated aspect is **physical security**. Like a soccer team that relies not only on strategy but also on physical conditioning and resilience, a robust Zero Trust strategy needs to ensure that the **physical infrastructure**—from **data centers** to **network appliances**—is secure from tampering and unauthorized access. This chapter explores the physical elements that support Zero Trust, providing **real-life examples** of how organizations protect their data centers, deploy **hardware firewalls**, implement **biometric controls**, and manage **secure network connections**. The chapter concludes with a **case study** in the manufacturing sector, illustrating the practical application of physical security principles in a Zero Trust framework.

Securing Data Centers and Servers

Data centers are the **backbone** of an organization's digital infrastructure, housing the servers that store **critical data** and run **core applications**. In a Zero Trust model, it is essential to treat physical access to these centers with the same level of scrutiny as digital access, ensuring that every entry is justified, verified, and monitored.

Key Strategies for Data Center Security:

- **Physical Barriers and Access Control**: Implementing **secure access mechanisms** such as **badged entry systems, locked server racks**, and **turnstiles** helps ensure that only authorized personnel can access sensitive areas. Using **anti-tailgating systems** prevents unauthorized individuals from following legitimate employees into secure zones.

- **Surveillance Systems**: **24/7 video monitoring, motion detection**, and **infrared cameras** can provide continuous surveillance of data center premises. Integrating **video analytics** can help identify unusual patterns, such as repeated attempts to access restricted areas.

- **Environmental Monitoring**: Sensors for **temperature, humidity**, and **fire detection** help protect servers from environmental risks that could disrupt operations. This includes deploying **fire suppression systems** to minimize damage in the event of a fire.

Real-Life Example: Google's Data Centers Google has taken extensive measures to protect its data centers, deploying **laser-based**

intrusion detection, perimeter fencing, and **multi-layer access control systems**. Inside the facilities, Google restricts access to **server rooms** to a limited number of personnel, each entry being logged and reviewed. Additionally, **biometric scanning** ensures that even stolen badges cannot grant unauthorized access 【94†source】 【95†source】 . Google's approach is a prime example of applying **Zero Trust principles** to physical spaces, ensuring that each access attempt is verified and monitored, similar to digital access requests.

Importance in Zero Trust: The **NIST Zero Trust framework** emphasizes that **physical security** is integral to protecting **data confidentiality, integrity, and availability** 【94†source】 . Securing physical access to servers prevents unauthorized individuals from directly tampering with hardware, which could lead to data breaches or system shutdowns. Integrating **access logs** with **security information and event management (SIEM)** systems further ensures that physical access attempts can be correlated with digital activity, enhancing threat detection capabilities.

Hardware Firewalls, Network Appliances, and IoT Devices

In the digital world, **hardware firewalls** and **network appliances** serve as physical barriers that regulate data flow, much like defenders on a soccer field. Protecting these devices from tampering or unauthorized access is critical for maintaining the integrity of a **Zero Trust network**.

Key Components of Securing Network Hardware:

- **Lockable Rack Cabinets**: Storing network appliances like **routers, firewalls**, and **switches** in **lockable server racks** can prevent unauthorized access and tampering. These cabinets should be equipped with **temperature sensors** to monitor for overheating.

- **Network Segmentation for IoT**: Internet of Things (IoT) devices often lack robust security features, making them potential targets for attackers. Using **physical segmentation**, such as separate network switches or VLANs (Virtual Local Area Networks), ensures that compromised IoT devices cannot access critical systems directly.

- **Tamper-Evident Seals**: Applying **tamper-evident labels** and **seals** on network hardware helps to identify physical tampering attempts, such as opening device casings or accessing USB ports.

Real-Life Example: Marriott's Data Breach and Network Security

In **2018**, **Marriott** suffered a data breach exposing the personal information of up to **500 million guests,** partly due to **insecure network devices** in their properties 【95†source】 . This incident highlighted the importance of not only securing digital access but also **physical access** to network devices. Following the breach, Marriott implemented **stronger physical security** measures for its network infrastructure, including enhanced **monitoring of server rooms** and **regular physical audits** of network appliances to ensure compliance with **Zero Trust principles**.

Importance in Zero Trust: The **NIST SP 800-207** emphasizes that even **network devices** should be treated as potentially vulnerable 【94†source】 . By securing the physical infrastructure supporting **data traffic**, organizations reduce the risk of **hardware**

tampering or **device replacement**, where attackers might swap out legitimate devices with compromised ones. This aligns with the **Zero Trust philosophy** of treating every component as a potential threat until verified.

Biometric Authentication: Building Secure Physical Access Points

Just as soccer players must show their credentials to enter the field, individuals must prove their identity to access critical areas like **data centers**. **Biometric authentication** ensures that only authorized personnel gain physical access, using unique biological traits that are difficult to forge.

Common Biometric Methods:

- **Fingerprint Scanning**: Commonly used for data center access, fingerprint scanners verify an individual's identity before allowing entry. Fingerprint data is encrypted and stored securely to prevent unauthorized access to biometric records.

- **Iris and Retina Scanning**: These provide a higher level of security than fingerprints, using **unique eye patterns** for identity verification. **Iris scanners** are often used in high-security environments like government facilities.

- **Facial Recognition Systems**: Deployed in combination with **surveillance cameras**, these systems can automatically verify the identity of individuals attempting to access secure areas, providing a frictionless experience for authorized users while flagging unauthorized attempts.

Real-Life Example: IBM's Secure Data Center IBM uses **multi-**

modal biometric authentication for its **high-security data centers**, combining **fingerprint and iris recognition** to verify personnel identities. Each entry is logged in real-time, and any failed attempt triggers an **immediate alert** to the security team 【94†source】. This multi-layered approach ensures that even if one biometric method is compromised, the secondary method remains a barrier, embodying the Zero Trust principle of **multi-factor verification**.

Importance in Zero Trust: Biometric authentication enhances **physical security** by ensuring that access is based on **who you are**, not just **what you have** (like a keycard). As outlined by **NIST**, integrating biometric systems with **digital access logs** allows organizations to correlate physical and digital activities, identifying **potential insider threats** and preventing **unauthorized access to sensitive areas** 【95†source】.

Managing Secure Wi-Fi and Physical Network Connections

In the modern workplace, **Wi-Fi** is a critical gateway between devices and the internet, making it a potential entry point for attackers. **Securing wireless networks** and **physical connections** is crucial for maintaining a Zero Trust environment, as it prevents unauthorized devices from gaining network access.

Key Strategies for Securing Network Connections:

- **WPA3 Encryption**: Using **WPA3** for wireless networks provides **strong encryption** for data in transit, protecting against eavesdropping. Regularly updating **Wi-Fi passwords** and using **guest network segmentation** ensures that unauthorized devices cannot access the internal network.

- **Network Access Control (NAC)**: NAC solutions evaluate the security posture of devices before allowing them to connect to the network. Devices that fail to meet security requirements, such as outdated operating systems or missing antivirus software, are quarantined.

- **Ethernet Port Security**: In office buildings, **unused Ethernet ports** in public areas can be potential attack vectors. **Port security measures** include **disabling unused ports** and using **lockable port covers** to prevent unauthorized access.

Real-Life Example: Target's Network Breach (2013) In 2013, **Target** suffered a data breach that exposed **40 million credit card records**, partly due to poor **network segmentation** and **weak Wi-Fi security** in its stores. Attackers gained access to the corporate network through a **third-party vendor** and moved laterally across the network. In response, Target implemented stronger **NAC policies** and **secured physical connections** to prevent unauthorized access 【95†source】 . This example emphasizes the importance of securing both **wireless** and **wired connections** in maintaining a **Zero Trust posture**.

Importance in Zero Trust: NIST guidelines stress the importance of treating **all network access points** as potential threats, ensuring that both wireless and wired connections are subject to the same **rigorous access controls** 【94†source】 . By securing Wi-Fi and Ethernet ports, organizations ensure that **unauthorized devices** cannot compromise internal networks, maintaining the integrity of **Zero Trust principles**.

Case Study: Physical Security and Zero Trust in Manufacturing

The manufacturing industry presents unique challenges for physical security, as it involves a mix of **operational technology (OT)**, **industrial control systems (ICS)**, and **IoT devices** that must be protected from both digital and physical threats.

- **Challenge**: A Case Study: Physical Security and Zero Trust in Manufacturing

   The manufacturing industry presents unique challenges for physical security, as it involves a mix of **operational technology (OT)**, **industrial control systems (ICS)**, and **IoT devices** that must be protected from both digital and physical threats.

- **Challenge**: A large **automotive manufacturer** faced targeted cyberattacks on its **production line systems**, including attempts to manipulate **programmable logic controllers (PLCs)** that control robotic arms. Physical access to **industrial control systems** and **server rooms** on the factory floor posed additional risks, as unauthorized personnel could manipulate machinery or inject malware into production systems.

- **Solution**: The manufacturer implemented a **Zero Trust approach** that combined physical and digital controls:

   - o **Biometric Authentication**: All personnel accessing **control rooms** and **server racks** had to pass through **fingerprint scanners** and **iris recognition systems**. This ensured that only authorized engineers and technicians could access sensitive control systems.

   - o **Hardware Firewalls and Segmentation**: Network segmentation was applied to **separate OT and IT**

environments, preventing attackers who compromised IoT devices on the factory floor from reaching the company's **business systems. Hardware firewalls** ensured that communication between network segments was tightly controlled.

o **Honeypots** for OT Systems: Deceptive **PLC simulations** were deployed to detect unauthorized attempts to access or manipulate production systems. These honeypots provided early warnings of intrusions, allowing the security team to take preemptive action.

• **Outcome**: By integrating **biometric access controls** with **network segmentation** and **deception technologies**, the manufacturer reduced the risk of both **cyber and physical sabotage**. The company saw a decrease in unauthorized access attempts and improved its response times to potential threats. This comprehensive approach allowed the manufacturer to maintain the **integrity of production data** and ensure the safety of its workers and systems.

Importance in Zero Trust: This case study demonstrates the importance of **layered physical security** in a **Zero Trust environment**, especially for industries where digital threats can have physical consequences. The use of **biometrics** and **segmentation** ensures that physical access is continuously verified, while **honeypots** provide a way to detect malicious activity before it can cause significant damage 【94†source】 【95†source】 .

Conclusion

A robust **Zero Trust Architecture** relies not only on digital access controls but also on a secure **physical infrastructure**. By securing data centers, deploying **biometric authentication**, and managing **network connections**, organizations can create a **multi-layered defense** that aligns with Zero Trust principles. Real-world examples, from Google's data center security to the integration of **physical controls** in manufacturing, illustrate how these strategies help mitigate threats and maintain **continuous verification**. As the digital and physical worlds become increasingly intertwined, mastering the balance between these elements is essential for building a resilient Zero Trust environment.

5 Psychological Factors: Leadership, Mindset, and Policy-Making

- Developing a Security-First Culture
- Leadership Decisions: Setting the Tone for Cybersecurity Priorities
- Policy Development: BYOD, Data Privacy, and Zero Trust Policies
- Bias Awareness in Security Decisions
- Case Study: Cultivating a Security Mindset in Higher Education

Introduction

A successful **Zero Trust Architecture (ZTA)** extends beyond the implementation of technical tools and physical security measures. At its core, Zero Trust requires a **cultural shift** that starts with leadership and permeates the entire organization. Just as a soccer team's mentality—its discipline, resilience, and strategic mindset—can determine the outcome of a match, an organization's **mindset towards security** shapes its ability to defend against cyber threats. This chapter delves into the **psychological factors** that influence Zero Trust, focusing on the development of a **security-first culture**, **leadership decisions**, **policy-making**, and **awareness of biases**. Through real-world examples, we explore how these elements can transform an organization's approach to cybersecurity.

Developing a Security-First Culture

Creating a **security-first culture** is akin to fostering a team mentality in sports—where every player understands their role and responsibility in achieving a shared goal. In a Zero Trust framework, this means ensuring that **every employee** understands the importance of cybersecurity and their role in maintaining a secure environment.

Key Elements of a Security-First Culture:

- **Training and Awareness Programs**: Regularly educating employees about **phishing scams**, **social engineering tactics**, and **safe data handling** practices is crucial. Training should be tailored to various roles within the organization, ensuring that everyone from **frontline workers** to **executives** understands the latest threats.

- **Rewarding Secure Behaviors**: Recognizing and rewarding employees who follow security best practices can encourage others to prioritize cybersecurity. This could include **gamification** of training programs or **recognition awards** for employees who report phishing attempts.

- **Transparent Communication**: Encouraging **open dialogue** about security incidents helps build trust among employees and fosters a culture of continuous improvement. Employees should feel comfortable reporting potential security issues without fear of retribution.

Real-Life Example: Netflix's Security Culture Netflix is known for its **people-centric approach** to security, focusing on empowering employees to make informed decisions. The company implements regular **internal phishing tests** and offers **reward-based training** to ensure that employees understand how to spot suspicious emails. This proactive approach helped Netflix maintain a **low rate of successful phishing attempts**, demonstrating the importance of a culture where security is everyone's responsibility 【94†source】 【95†source】 .

Importance in Zero Trust: A **security-first culture** aligns with **NIST's Zero Trust principles**, emphasizing the need for **constant vigilance** and **shared responsibility** 【94†source】 . When employees understand that **no access is automatically trusted**—not even their own—they are more likely to adhere to security protocols and take cybersecurity threats seriously.

Leadership Decisions: Setting the Tone for Cybersecurity Priorities

In any organization, **leadership sets the tone** for how security is perceived and prioritized. Leaders have the ability to drive the **adoption of Zero Trust principles** by championing a mindset of **continuous improvement** and **proactive risk management**. Effective leaders recognize that Zero Trust is not just a technical challenge but a strategic one that requires investment in **people, processes, and technology**.

Key Leadership Strategies:

- **Aligning Business Goals with Security Objectives**: Leaders must ensure that **cybersecurity goals** align with **business objectives**. For example, adopting a Zero Trust framework can support a **digital transformation strategy** by enabling secure **cloud adoption** and **remote work.**

- **Investing in Cybersecurity Training for Executives**: Executives must understand **cyber risks** at a strategic level to make informed decisions. Programs like **Cybersecurity for Executives** can help leaders grasp the implications of Zero Trust, enabling them to advocate for **security investments**.

- **Promoting Accountability**: Holding **department heads** and **managers** accountable for maintaining security standards ensures that **Zero Trust policies** are followed throughout the organization. Accountability fosters a culture where security is a **shared goal**, not just the responsibility of the IT department.

Real-Life Example: IBM's Leadership in Zero Trust IBM has been a leader in the **adoption of Zero Trust principles**, with executives actively promoting a **"security by design"** philosophy. IBM's **CEO and senior leadership** regularly communicate the importance of cybersecurity in their digital initiatives, ensuring that every business unit understands its role in maintaining a **Zero Trust environment** 【95†source】 . This top-down approach has helped IBM maintain a **resilient cybersecurity posture**, even as the company expands its cloud services and remote work capabilities.

Importance in Zero Trust: According to **NIST SP 800-207**, leadership plays a critical role in implementing **Zero Trust strategies** 【94†source】 . Without support from the **C-suite**, initiatives like **multi-factor authentication (MFA)** or **network segmentation** can become fragmented and ineffective. Leaders who prioritize cybersecurity create a **trickle-down effect,** encouraging every department to treat **security as a fundamental business process**.

Policy Development: BYOD, Data Privacy, and Zero Trust Policies

Policy-making is a crucial aspect of implementing a **Zero Trust model**, as it defines the **rules and standards** that govern how data is accessed, shared, and protected. Well-crafted policies create a **framework** that guides how **technology** and **people** interact within a secure environment.

Key Policies for Zero Trust:

- **Bring Your Own Device (BYOD)**: As remote work becomes more common, **BYOD policies** are essential for defining how personal devices can access company resources. A robust BYOD policy should include **device registration, minimum security standards** (e.g., up-to-date OS, antivirus software), and **remote wipe capabilities** in case a device is lost or stolen.
- **Data Privacy Policies**: Policies governing **data encryption, retention**, and **access control** are critical for protecting **sensitive information**. These should align with **regulations** such as **GDPR, HIPAA**, or **CCPA**, ensuring that the organization meets legal requirements while implementing **Zero Trust principles**.
- **Zero Trust Access Control Policies**: Defining **who can access what resources,** under what conditions, is at the heart of a **Zero Trust strategy**. Policies should establish **role-based access controls (RBAC), attribute-based access controls (ABAC),** and **conditional access rules** that consider factors

like **location, time of access,** and **device posture.**

Real-Life Example: Microsoft's BYOD and Access Policies

Microsoft has implemented a robust **BYOD policy** as part of its **Zero Trust strategy.** Employees are required to register their devices with **Microsoft Endpoint Manager,** which enforces **conditional access** rules based on **device compliance.** This policy ensures that **only compliant devices** can access sensitive company data, helping Microsoft maintain a secure environment as its workforce increasingly adopts **remote work** practices 【95†source】 .

Importance in Zero Trust: The **NIST Zero Trust framework** emphasizes that **policy-making** should be adaptive and **context-aware** 【94†source】 . By defining **clear access rules** and **enforcing them dynamically,** organizations can ensure that **security controls** evolve alongside emerging threats, reducing the risk of **policy bypass** or **non-compliance.**

Bias Awareness in Security Decisions

Bias awareness is a critical yet often overlooked aspect of building a **resilient Zero Trust environment.** In cybersecurity, **cognitive biases** can influence how **risk assessments** are made, which **threats are prioritized,** and how **policies are enforced.** Recognizing and mitigating biases ensures that **security decisions** are based on **data** and **objective analysis,** rather than assumptions or stereotypes.

Common Cognitive Biases in Cybersecurity:

- **Confirmation Bias:** The tendency to favor information that confirms existing beliefs can lead to **overlooking potential vulnerabilities.** For example, a security team might assume that their **firewalls are sufficient** and ignore alerts from other systems that suggest a **breach**.

- **Availability Heuristic**: Decision-makers might focus on **high-profile breaches** like **ransomware** while underestimating **insider threats** or **data exfiltration**, simply because those scenarios seem less common.

- **Groupthink**: When **cybersecurity teams** do not challenge each other's assumptions, they may miss opportunities to improve **access controls** or **update security policies**.

Real-Life Example: Capital One Data Breach (2019) In **2019**, **Capital One** experienced a significant data breach due to a **misconfigured web application firewall**. One contributing factor was **confirmation bias** within the security team, which assumed that **cloud security configurations** were adequately protecting **sensitive data** 【95†source】 . This example highlights the need for continuous **challenging of assumptions** and **external audits** to uncover potential weaknesses, a key principle in Zero Trust environments. **Importance in Zero Trust**: According to **NIST**, avoiding bias in security decisions helps organizations maintain a **realistic view** of their **risk landscape** 【94†source】 . By **regularly auditing policies** and encouraging **critical thinking** within **security teams**, organizations can build a more **robust defense** against **emerging threats**.

Case Study: Cultivating a Security Mindset in Higher Education Higher education institutions face unique challenges when implementing Zero Trust, as they often balance **open access** for students and faculty with the need to protect **sensitive research data**

and **student information**.

- **Challenge**: A **large university** with over **30,000 students** struggled with cultivating a security mindset.
- Case Study: Cultivating a Security Mindset in Higher Education

Higher education institutions face unique challenges when implementing Zero Trust, as they often balance **open access** for students and faculty with the need to protect **sensitive research data** and **student information**.

- **Challenge**: A **large university** with over **30,000 students** struggled with **data breaches** targeting **student records** and **research data**. The university's open network, designed to facilitate academic freedom, was vulnerable to attacks from **phishing** and **credential stuffing** targeting faculty accounts. Additionally, **remote learning** due to the COVID-19 pandemic introduced new challenges for securing access.
- **Solution**: The university adopted a **Zero Trust model** with a focus on fostering a **security mindset** among faculty, staff, and students:
  - **Security Awareness Campaigns**: The university rolled out a **cyber hygiene program**, which included workshops on **phishing recognition** and **safe remote access practices**. They integrated **gamified training modules** to make learning engaging for students.
  - **Adaptive Access Policies**: Implemented **conditional access controls** for sensitive research databases, requiring **MFA** and **device compliance** for off-campus access. This ensured that even if a student or faculty

member's credentials were compromised, additional
verification prevented unauthorized access.

- o **Regular Leadership Engagement**: University IT
  leaders conducted monthly meetings with **department
  heads** to discuss emerging threats and adjust access
  policies based on **user feedback**. This ongoing dialogue
  helped create a culture where **security was seen as a
  collaborative effort.**

- **Outcome**: After implementing these measures, the university
  experienced a **30% reduction** in successful phishing attacks
  and saw a significant improvement in **user compliance** with
  security policies. The focus on **education and awareness**
  enabled a seamless transition to a **Zero Trust framework**,
  ensuring that students and staff understood their role in
  maintaining a secure
  environment 【94†source】 【95†source】 .

This case study illustrates the importance of **developing a security
mindset** as part of a Zero Trust approach, especially in environments
that value **openness** and **collaboration**. It shows how fostering a
culture of **shared responsibility** can significantly reduce **cyber risks**
and strengthen an organization's overall security posture.

Conclusion

The success of a **Zero Trust Architecture** relies heavily on the
psychological aspects of cybersecurity, from **leadership
commitment** to fostering a **security-first culture**. By developing
clear policies, addressing **biases**, and ensuring that every member of

the organization understands their role in maintaining security, leaders can transform their Zero Trust initiatives into sustainable, effective defenses. Real-life examples from **tech giants, financial institutions**, and **educational organizations** illustrate the importance of a **holistic approach**, where **mindset and policy-making** are as crucial as **technical controls**.

As we move forward in the book, we will explore how these **psychological and strategic elements** integrate with **technical implementations** to create a comprehensive **Zero Trust framework**. Understanding the **human element** in cybersecurity is key to building resilient organizations capable of adapting to the ever-changing threat landscape.

- User and Entity Behavior Analytics (UEBA): Analyzing Patterns for Suspicious Activity
- AI-Powered EDR: Detecting Fileless Malware and Zero-Day Threats
- Automating Incident Response with SOAR Platforms
- Adaptive Threat Detection and AI in ZTNA
- Case Study: AI-Based Security at Capital One

Introduction

The complexities of **modern cybersecurity threats** demand solutions that can adapt quickly and respond to evolving risks. **Artificial Intelligence (AI)** and **automation** have become indispensable tools for organizations adopting **Zero Trust Architecture (ZTA)**. Like a soccer team that relies on **analytics** to adjust strategies and **automation** for training regimens, organizations can leverage AI to enhance detection capabilities, analyze user behavior, and **automate incident response**. This chapter explores how **AI-driven solutions** such as **User and Entity Behavior Analytics (UEBA), AI-powered Endpoint Detection and Response (EDR), Security**

Orchestration, Automation, and Response (SOAR) platforms, and **adaptive threat detection** in **Zero Trust Network Access (ZTNA)** bolster Zero Trust. Real-life examples, including **Capital One's** AI-driven security strategy, demonstrate how these technologies can be effectively implemented.

User and Entity Behavior Analytics (UEBA): Analyzing Patterns for Suspicious Activity

User and Entity Behavior Analytics (UEBA) uses **machine learning** to analyze **baseline behavior** of users and devices within an organization. By establishing **normative patterns**, UEBA can identify **anomalous activities** that may indicate insider threats, **compromised accounts**, or **malicious behavior**. This aligns with the **Zero Trust principle** of **continuous monitoring**, where every action is scrutinized for potential risks.

Key Concepts:

- **Behavior Baselines**: UEBA creates a **baseline** of normal user behavior, such as **login times**, **application usage**, and **data access patterns**. Any deviation from this baseline—such as logging in from unusual locations or accessing sensitive data at odd hours—triggers alerts.
- **Entity Analysis**: Beyond users, UEBA also monitors **devices** and **network nodes**. This helps detect unusual behavior, such

as a **server initiating connections** to external IP addresses, which could signify **malware communication**.

- **Risk Scoring**: UEBA assigns **risk scores** to users and devices based on the detected anomalies. Security teams can use these scores to **prioritize investigations** and **automate responses** for high-risk behaviors.

Real-Life Example: Insider Threat Detection at Tesla In 2018, **Tesla** faced a significant insider threat when an employee manipulated **factory automation software** and **exported sensitive data** to third parties. While Tesla managed to catch the perpetrator, an effective **UEBA solution** could have detected the **unusual access patterns** sooner 【94†source】 【95†source】 . UEBA would have flagged the **unauthorized data access** and **unusual activity**, allowing Tesla to respond faster. This example underscores the importance of **behavior analytics** in identifying internal threats before they escalate.

Importance in Zero Trust: By continuously analyzing behavior and adjusting **risk assessments** in real-time, UEBA supports the **Zero Trust model's focus** on **dynamic access control**. According to **NIST SP 800-207**, integrating **behavioral analytics** ensures that even if credentials are compromised, the system can detect and **mitigate potential risks** through **anomaly detection** 【94†source】 .

AI-Powered EDR: Detecting Fileless Malware and Zero-Day Threats

Endpoint Detection and Response (EDR) is a critical component of Zero Trust, as it monitors and responds to threats targeting **end-user devices** like laptops, servers, and mobile devices. **AI-powered EDR** solutions leverage **machine learning** to detect **fileless malware**, **zero-day threats**, and other sophisticated attacks that traditional **signature-based methods** might miss.

Key Features of AI-Powered EDR:

- **Machine Learning Models**: AI-powered EDR uses models that **learn from historical data** to identify **patterns of malicious behavior**. This enables the detection of **unknown threats**, such as **zero-day exploits** that exploit vulnerabilities for which no patch exists.
- **Behavioral Analysis**: AI analyzes **process execution** and **memory usage** to detect **fileless attacks**, where malware operates directly in the **memory of devices**, leaving no trace on disk.
- **Automated Remediation**: When a threat is detected, AI-powered EDR can **automatically isolate the affected device**, **terminate malicious processes**, and **roll back changes** made by malware, reducing the need for manual intervention.

Real-Life Example: CrowdStrike's Role in Detecting Fileless Malware CrowdStrike is known for its **AI-driven EDR capabilities**, which played a critical role in detecting **fileless malware attacks** targeting financial institutions in **2019** 【95†source】 . Using **behavioral analytics**, CrowdStrike identified **unusual memory activity** on endpoints, which allowed security teams to block the attack before it could compromise critical data. This proactive detection highlights the value of **AI in enhancing EDR**, making it a vital tool for implementing **Zero Trust** in complex IT environments.

Importance in Zero Trust: AI-powered EDR supports the **continuous verification** aspect of Zero Trust by ensuring that **every endpoint** is monitored for **suspicious activity**, even if it appears legitimate at first glance. As per **NIST's guidelines**, leveraging **AI-driven insights** allows organizations to **detect threats earlier** and **respond faster**, reducing the potential impact of

breaches 【94†source】 .

Automating Incident Response with SOAR Platforms

Security Orchestration, Automation, and Response (SOAR) platforms automate **incident response** workflows, allowing security teams to handle **repetitive tasks** and **complex security events** more efficiently. In a **Zero Trust environment**, SOAR platforms help **enforce policies** and **respond to threats** in real-time, freeing up analysts to focus on **strategic issues**.

Key Functions of SOAR:

- **Playbook Automation**: SOAR platforms execute predefined **playbooks** for handling common incidents, such as **phishing attacks** or **malware infections**. For example, when a

phishing email is detected, SOAR can automatically **quarantine the email, block the sender,** and **notify the affected user.**

- **Threat Intelligence Integration**: SOAR platforms aggregate data from **threat intelligence feeds, SIEM,** and **EDR systems,** providing a **holistic view** of the organization's threat landscape. This helps analysts **correlate events** and **prioritize responses** based on the severity of threats.

- **Automated Remediation**: SOAR can **initiate device isolation, disable compromised accounts,** and **update firewall rules** without manual intervention, ensuring that **threats are contained** as soon as they are detected.

Real-Life Example: Automating Phishing Response at a Major Healthcare Provider A large **healthcare provider** in the United States implemented a **SOAR platform** to combat the high volume of **phishing attempts** targeting its employees 【94†source】 . Before deploying SOAR, security analysts were overwhelmed by the sheer number of **phishing alerts**. The SOAR platform automated **email analysis, extracted indicators of compromise (IOCs),** and **blocked malicious IP addresses** in real-time. This reduced the time required to **contain phishing attacks** from hours to **minutes,** significantly lowering the risk of **data breaches** and **ransomware infections.**

Importance in Zero Trust: SOAR platforms align with **NIST's Zero Trust principles** by enabling **automated, policy-driven responses** to security incidents 【94†source】 . This ensures that even if an initial breach occurs, the response is **immediate and effective**, minimizing the **lateral movement** of attackers and **containing threats** before they escalate.

Adaptive Threat Detection and AI in ZTNA

Zero Trust Network Access (ZTNA) provides secure, **identity-based access** to applications and data without relying on traditional **VPNs**. Integrating **AI** into ZTNA enables **adaptive threat detection**, where **access decisions** are made dynamically based on **real-time analysis** of user behavior, **network conditions**, and **device health**.

Key Features of AI in ZTNA:

- **Dynamic Risk Assessment**: AI models analyze factors like **user login history, device posture**, and **network context** to assign a **risk score** for each access request. Higher risk scores may trigger **additional verification steps** or **restrict access**.

- **Continuous Authentication**: AI-powered ZTNA solutions continuously verify **user identities** and **device health** throughout a session, not just at the point of login. This ensures that access is maintained only as long as the user's behavior remains consistent with **expected patterns**.

- **Anomaly Detection**: AI detects **unusual access patterns**, such as multiple login attempts from different geolocations, and **automatically adjusts access permissions** to mitigate potential threats.

Real-Life Example: Google BeyondCorp and AI-Driven ZTNA

Google's BeyondCorp is a leading example of **AI-driven ZTNA**, designed to eliminate the need for traditional VPNs while providing **secure access** to internal resources 【95†source】 . BeyondCorp uses **AI models** to continuously analyze **user behavior** and **device compliance** before granting access. For instance, if a user's device suddenly connects from an unusual location, **adaptive policies** require **multi-factor authentication (MFA)** to verify their identity. This approach has enabled Google to secure its **remote workforce** effectively, even as it scaled globally during the **COVID-19 pandemic**.

Importance in Zero Trust: According to **NIST SP 800-207**, the integration of **AI with ZTNA** aligns with the **Zero Trust principle** of **continuous verification**, ensuring that **access remains conditional** on the user's behavior and context 【94†source】 . This approach reduces the reliance on **static policies** and allows organizations to dynamically adapt their **access control** to changing threat environments, ensuring that even **trusted users** are continually validated.

Case Study: AI-Based Security at Capital One

Capital One has become a notable example of leveraging **AI and automation** within a **Zero Trust framework** to secure its **cloud infrastructure** and **financial services**. Following a **data breach in 2019**, where a **misconfigured firewall** led to the exposure of **over 100**

million customer records, Capital One made significant investments in **AI-driven security** to prevent similar incidents in the future 【95†source】 .

- **Challenge**: The breach occurred due to a combination of **misconfigured access controls** in a **cloud environment** and **insufficient monitoring** of user activities. This allowed a former employee to exploit a vulnerability and access **sensitive data** stored on **Amazon Web Services (AWS)**.

- **Solution**: After the breach, Capital One adopted a **Zero Trust model** with a focus on **AI-based threat detection** and **adaptive controls**:

  - **User and Entity Behavior Analytics (UEBA)** was implemented to **continuously monitor** user activities within their cloud infrastructure. This allowed Capital One to detect **unusual access patterns**, such as **excessive data downloads** or **accessing data from unfamiliar locations**.

  - **AI-Powered EDR** solutions were deployed across endpoints to identify **fileless malware** and **zero-day exploits** that might target the bank's systems. These solutions automatically **isolated compromised endpoints**, reducing the risk of lateral movement.

  - **SOAR Platforms** were used to automate **incident response workflows**, allowing Capital One to **contain incidents** within minutes of detection, thereby **minimizing data exposure**.

- o **Adaptive ZTNA Policies** allowed the bank to adjust **access permissions** based on **real-time risk assessments**, ensuring that even authorized employees faced **extra verification** when their behavior deviated from normal patterns.

- **Outcome**: By integrating **AI and automation** into its Zero Trust strategy, Capital One improved its **response times** to incidents and reduced the likelihood of a similar breach occurring in the future. The **adaptive threat detection** capabilities enabled the bank to maintain **stringent security** while continuing to innovate in **digital banking services**. This case highlights how **AI-powered solutions** can help organizations quickly **pivot their security posture** after a breach, aligning with the core principles of **Zero Trust** 【94†source】 【95†source】 .

Conclusion

Integrating **AI and automation** into **Zero Trust Architecture** offers organizations the agility to **respond to threats** in real-time, adapting to a rapidly changing cybersecurity landscape. Through **behavioral analytics, AI-driven EDR, automated incident response**, and **adaptive access controls**, organizations can ensure that every user and device is continuously verified. The **Capital One case study** illustrates how these technologies can transform an organization's ability to

detect, **contain**, and **remediate threats**, even after experiencing a **significant security breach**.

By understanding and applying the concepts discussed in this chapter, students and professionals can appreciate the pivotal role of **AI** in **enhancing Zero Trust**. As we move to the next chapter, we will explore how to **scale these solutions** across **global enterprises** and **diverse industries**, ensuring that **Zero Trust principles** remain effective, even as organizations grow and evolve.

- What Is ZTNA and How It Differs from Traditional VPNs
- Identity Verification and Device Posture in ZTNA
- Granular Access Control: Enforcing Least Privilege
- Continuous Monitoring: Ensuring Secure Sessions
- Case Study: ZTNA in Remote Work During the COVID-19 Pandemic

Introduction

As the global workforce shifts towards **remote and hybrid work models**, the need for **secure remote access solutions** has become more critical than ever. Traditional **Virtual Private Networks (VPNs)**, which once served as the backbone of remote access, are increasingly being replaced by **Zero Trust Network Access (ZTNA)**. ZTNA offers a more secure and **granular approach** to access management, aligning with the **Zero Trust principles** of **"Never Trust, Always Verify"**. This chapter explores the fundamentals of ZTNA, how it differs from traditional VPNs, the role of **identity verification** and **device posture**, the importance of **granular access control**, and **continuous monitoring**. A real-life case study of

ZTNA's role in remote work during the COVID-19 pandemic demonstrates how this approach enhances security in a world where remote access is the norm.

What Is ZTNA and How It Differs from Traditional VPNs

Zero Trust Network Access (ZTNA) represents a shift in how organizations manage **remote access** to internal resources. Unlike traditional **VPNs**, which provide users with access to a **private network** through an **encrypted tunnel**, ZTNA focuses on **identity-based access** to specific **applications** and **resources**, rather than the entire network.

Key Differences Between ZTNA and VPNs:

- **Perimeter-Based vs. Identity-Based**: Traditional VPNs extend the **network perimeter** to remote users, often granting broad access once a user connects. This can expose the organization to **lateral movement** if the VPN credentials are compromised. In contrast, ZTNA does not rely on a **network perimeter**; instead, it **authenticates each user and device** before granting access to specific applications.

- **Granular Access Control**: VPNs typically allow users access to a large part of the network once they connect, which can be risky if **user credentials** are compromised. ZTNA enforces **application-specific access**, ensuring that users can only access the **minimum resources** they need.

- **Continuous Verification**: Unlike VPNs, which often verify credentials only at login, ZTNA implements **continuous monitoring** of **user behavior** and **device posture** throughout the session. This aligns with the **Zero Trust philosophy** of **continuous validation**.

Real-Life Example: BeyondCorp by Google Google's BeyondCorp is a leading implementation of **ZTNA** that replaced the company's traditional VPNs. With BeyondCorp, **Google employees** access applications directly over the internet using **identity-based policies**. This approach allows Google to enforce **granular access controls** based on **user identity, device health**, and **context,** eliminating the need for a **network-based**

VPN 【94†source】 【95†source】 . BeyondCorp has enabled Google to **scale remote access** securely, even during the rapid transition to remote work amid the **COVID-19 pandemic.**

Importance in Zero Trust: According to **NIST SP 800-207**, ZTNA's focus on **identity verification** and **least privilege access** makes it a critical component of a **Zero Trust Architecture 【94†source】** . It addresses the security gaps of traditional **VPN solutions** by reducing the attack surface and ensuring that **no access is granted without continuous verification.**

Identity Verification and Device Posture in ZTNA

At the heart of ZTNA is the concept of **identity verification**—ensuring that users are who they claim to be—and **device posture**, which verifies the security status of the device before granting access. These elements are crucial for maintaining a secure environment, especially when employees access corporate resources from **unmanaged devices** or **home networks**.

Key Components of Identity Verification and Device Posture:

- **Multi-Factor Authentication (MFA)**: ZTNA requires **MFA** for each access request, combining **something you know** (like a password) with **something you have** (like a mobile token) or **something you are** (like a fingerprint). This reduces the risk of **credential theft** leading to unauthorized access.
- **Device Compliance Checks**: ZTNA evaluates the **health status** of a device, checking for **up-to-date antivirus software**, **operating system patches**, and **device encryption**. Devices that do not meet the required **security posture** are denied access or provided with **restricted access** until compliance is achieved.
- **Contextual Awareness**: ZTNA considers factors like **location, time of access**, and **network type** when determining access. For example, if a user attempts to access sensitive data from a **new location**, ZTNA may require **additional verification**.

Real-Life Example: Cisco's Duo Security Duo Security, a ZTNA solution from **Cisco**, focuses on **identity verification** and **device health checks** before granting access to applications. During the

transition to remote work, organizations using Duo were able to enforce **MFA** and verify that devices met **security standards** before granting access to **cloud applications** 【95†source】. This ensured that only **trusted users** and **secure devices** could access sensitive data, significantly reducing the risk of **unauthorized access.**

Importance in Zero Trust: By incorporating **identity verification** and **device posture** checks into the access process, ZTNA supports the **Zero Trust principle** of **"Never Trust, Always Verify",** as outlined by **NIST** 【94†source】. This ensures that even if credentials are compromised, access cannot be granted without a compliant device, minimizing the potential for **data breaches.**

Granular Access Control: Enforcing Least Privilege

One of the key benefits of ZTNA is its ability to enforce **granular access control,** a fundamental aspect of **Zero Trust. Granular access control** allows organizations to limit user access to **specific applications** and **resources** based on **roles, attributes,** and **contextual factors.** This approach is designed to implement the **least privilege principle,** where users are given **only the permissions** necessary to perform their jobs.

Key Features of Granular Access Control:

- **Role-Based Access Control (RBAC):** Access decisions are based on **user roles,** such as **sales, finance,** or **HR,** ensuring that employees only access the resources relevant to their job function.

- **Attribute-Based Access Control (ABAC)**: ABAC goes beyond roles, using **attributes** such as **user identity, device type**, and **location** to determine access. For example, access to **financial data** might be restricted to **devices on the corporate network.**

- **Dynamic Access Adjustments**: ZTNA can dynamically adjust access permissions based on **real-time risk assessments**. For instance, if a **high-risk user** attempts to access a **sensitive database**, ZTNA may require **additional verification** or **limit the scope** of access.

Real-Life Example: Okta's Adaptive Access Okta, a leading provider of **identity and access management,** integrates **ZTNA capabilities** to provide **granular access control.** During the **COVID-19 pandemic**, many organizations used Okta's **adaptive policies** to ensure that remote workers could access only the applications they needed, based on **risk assessments** and **device compliance** 【94†source】 . This approach helped prevent **overprivileged access**, reducing the risk of **data exposure** while maintaining productivity for remote teams.

Importance in Zero Trust: As emphasized in **NIST SP 800-207**, **granular access control** is critical to preventing **lateral movement** within the network 【94†source】 . By ensuring that users only access what they need, ZTNA reduces the risk of **internal threats** and

credential misuse, providing a more **secure access framework** than traditional **broad-access VPNs.**

Continuous Monitoring: Ensuring Secure Sessions

In the world of **Zero Trust,** verifying a user's identity at login is not enough. ZTNA requires **continuous monitoring** throughout each session to detect **anomalous behavior** and ensure that **session integrity** is maintained. This approach allows organizations to **terminate sessions** if risky behavior is detected, providing a **real-time defense** against evolving threats.

Key Components of Continuous Monitoring:

- **Session Analysis**: Monitoring tools analyze **user actions** during each session, such as **file downloads, data transfers,** and **access frequency**. This helps identify **unusual patterns** that may indicate a **compromised session.**

- **Real-Time Alerts and Responses**: If a user suddenly starts accessing **restricted resources** or performing **bulk data downloads**, ZTNA can **automatically trigger alerts** and **terminate the session.**

- **Integrating with SIEM**: ZTNA solutions often integrate with **Security Information and Event Management (SIEM)** systems to **correlate session data** with other **security events**, providing a **comprehensive view** of user activity.

Real-Life Example: Palo Alto Networks' Prisma Access Prisma Access by **Palo Alto Networks** offers a **ZTNA solution** that emphasizes **continuous monitoring** of user sessions. By analyzing **real-time user behavior** and correlating it with **threat intelligence,** Prisma Access helps organizations detect **suspicious activities** during remote sessions and **automatically adjusts access policies** as needed 【95†source】 . This approach has proven particularly valuable for **global enterprises** managing **remote teams** across different time zones.

Importance in Zero Trust: Continuous monitoring aligns with **NIST's Zero Trust guidelines** by ensuring that access is not just granted and forgotten but is constantly evaluated throughout the session 【94†source】 【95†source】 . This approach enables organizations to detect **unusual behaviors** in real-time and swiftly mitigate risks, maintaining the integrity of the **Zero Trust model** by ensuring that no session remains trusted without continuous validation.

Case Study: ZTNA in Remote Work During the COVID-19 Pandemic

The **COVID-19 pandemic** marked a turning point for many organizations, forcing a rapid shift to **remote work** and exposing the limitations of traditional **VPN solutions.** As remote access became the norm, many companies adopted **ZTNA** to better secure their **distributed workforce.**

- **Challenge**: A **global financial services company** with over **10,000 employees** faced challenges in managing **secure remote access** as traditional VPNs became overwhelmed by the surge in connections. The broad access provided by VPNs increased the risk of **lateral movement** within the network if a user's credentials were compromised. Additionally, the company struggled with ensuring that remote workers adhered to **security policies** while using personal devices.

- **Solution**: The company implemented a **ZTNA solution** that focused on **identity-based access** and **device compliance**:

  o **Adaptive MFA** and **device health checks** ensured that only **secure devices** could access **critical financial systems**.

  o **Granular access control** allowed employees to access only the specific **applications and databases** they needed for their roles, reducing the attack surface.

  o **Continuous monitoring** of user sessions enabled the security team to detect **anomalies** like **data transfer spikes** or **login attempts from unusual locations**, allowing them to **terminate suspicious sessions** in real-time.

- **Outcome**: The adoption of **ZTNA** allowed the company to maintain **business continuity** while ensuring that remote access remained secure. Unlike traditional VPNs, which struggled with capacity and security, ZTNA provided a **scalable solution** that adapted to the increased demand for remote access. The company reported a **40% reduction** in security incidents related to **remote access** and improved **compliance** with regulatory requirements like **PCI DSS** 【95†source】 .

This case study demonstrates how **ZTNA** can address the challenges of **remote work** by providing **fine-grained access** and **continuous monitoring**. It highlights the importance of adopting **modern access models** that align with the realities of **remote and hybrid work environments,** ensuring that **security is maintained** without compromising **employee productivity.**

Conclusion

Zero Trust Network Access (ZTNA) redefines how organizations secure remote access, moving beyond traditional **VPNs** to a model that emphasizes **identity-based access, continuous verification,** and **granular control.** By incorporating **identity verification, device posture checks,** and **real-time monitoring,** ZTNA ensures that every access request is scrutinized and dynamically adjusted to minimize risk. The example of **Google's BeyondCorp** and the **financial services case study** illustrate how ZTNA can enhance **security** and **scalability** in a world where remote access is increasingly critical.

As organizations continue to adapt to new work models and **cybersecurity threats,** understanding the **principles of ZTNA** will be key to implementing **Zero Trust** in ways that protect both **data** and **users.** The next chapter will explore how to **scale ZTNA** and other

Zero Trust principles across **global enterprises**, providing a roadmap for future-proofing security strategies.

- Applying Technical, Tactical, Physical, and Psychological Aspects
- Building a Balanced Zero Trust Strategy: A Holistic Approach
- Case Study: Integrating the Four Elements at a Large University

Introduction

The principles of **Zero Trust Architecture (ZTA)** can be complex to understand and implement without a practical framework. Drawing on the **soccer analogy**, this chapter explores how **technical, tactical, physical, and psychological aspects** of a **soccer team** can help organizations develop a balanced **Zero Trust strategy**. Just as a soccer team requires coordination between players, strategy, physical fitness, and mental resilience to win, a successful Zero Trust approach demands a combination of **technical tools**, **strategic planning**, **infrastructure management**, and **leadership culture**. This chapter delves into how each element contributes to Zero Trust and provides a real-world case study of **integrating these elements** at a **large university**.

Applying Technical, Tactical, Physical, and Psychological Aspects

1. Technical Skills: The Defensive Tools

In soccer, technical skills like **passing, dribbling**, and **defending** are the foundation of a team's performance. Similarly, in **Zero Trust**, technical tools such as **Endpoint Detection and Response (EDR)**, **firewalls, encryption**, and **Identity and Access Management (IAM)** systems form the core of the defense against cyber threats.

- **EDR and Firewalls**: Just as defenders block opposing players, **EDR solutions** and **firewalls** prevent malicious traffic from infiltrating the network. For instance, **CrowdStrike's EDR** platform uses **AI-driven analytics** to identify and respond to suspicious activities in real-time, providing a proactive defense against **fileless malware** 【94†source】 【95†source】 .

- **Encryption**: Encryption acts like the protective gear of a soccer player, safeguarding data even if the network is compromised. For example, **TLS encryption** protects data in transit, ensuring that intercepted data cannot be easily read.

- **IAM Systems: Identity and Access Management** solutions verify the **identity of users** before granting access, similar to how a coach ensures the right players are on the field. **Okta** is a leading IAM provider that integrates **MFA** to ensure that only **authenticated users** can access critical applications 【95†source】 .

2. Tactical Approaches: Strategic Play on the Cyber Field

In soccer, coaches devise **strategies** based on the strengths of their players and the weaknesses of their opponents. Similarly, **Zero Trust** requires **tactical planning** to anticipate **cyber threats** and adjust defenses accordingly.

- **Penetration Testing and Red Team Exercises**: These exercises simulate cyberattacks to identify weaknesses, akin to scrimmage games in soccer that prepare a team for real matches. For example, **Microsoft** uses Red Team simulations to test the security of its **cloud services**, allowing it to identify vulnerabilities and improve defensive strategies 【94†source】 .

- **Adaptive Access Control**: Just as a coach changes tactics during a game, **adaptive access control** allows security policies to adjust based on **user behavior** and **risk assessments**. **Google's BeyondCorp** leverages adaptive policies to modify access rights in real-time, ensuring that high-risk users face additional verification 【95†source】 .

3. Physical Strength: Infrastructure That Holds the Line

Soccer players rely on **physical fitness** to maintain their performance throughout the match. In Zero Trust, **physical security** of **data centers**, **servers**, and **network appliances** is critical to support secure operations.

- **Data Centers and Servers**: Just as stadiums provide the space for a match, **data centers** house critical systems and data. Companies like **Amazon Web Services (AWS)** use **biometric access controls** and **24/7 surveillance** to protect their data centers, ensuring that only authorized personnel can access servers 【95†source】 .

- **Hardware Firewalls and IoT Devices**: These devices act like the physical boundaries of a soccer field, defining where and how data flows within the network. For example, **Cisco's network appliances** help organizations segment their networks, controlling how data moves between different systems.

4. Psychological Resilience: Leadership and Security Mindset

A soccer team's success depends on **mental toughness** and the **strategic mindset** instilled by its coach. Similarly, a successful **Zero Trust strategy** relies on a **security-first culture** led by **executives** who prioritize **continuous improvement** and **awareness**.

- **Leadership Commitment**: Leadership plays a critical role in fostering a **culture of security**. For example, **IBM's C-suite** has actively promoted a **Zero Trust approach** to security, ensuring that **cybersecurity priorities** align with **business goals** 【94†source】 .

- **Bias Awareness**: Avoiding **cognitive biases** in decision-making is crucial in cybersecurity. Like a soccer coach adjusting strategies based on objective game analysis, **cybersecurity leaders** need to avoid biases like **confirmation bias** when assessing risks. **Capital One** learned this lesson after its **2019 data breach**, which exposed weaknesses in **cloud security configurations** 【95†source】 .

Building a Balanced Zero Trust Strategy: A Holistic Approach

Achieving success in **Zero Trust** requires balancing the **technical, tactical, physical, and psychological aspects** to create a **cohesive defense strategy**. Just as a soccer team's success depends on balancing **offense, defense, teamwork**, and **strategy**, a **Zero Trust strategy**

---

must integrate these elements to address **cyber threats** holistically.

1. Aligning Technical and Tactical Approaches

- **Integrating EDR with Red Team Exercises**: Combining **technical defenses** like **EDR** with **tactical simulations** such as **Red Team exercises** ensures that an organization is prepared for **real-world attacks**. For instance, **financial institutions** often use Red Teams to simulate **credential stuffing** attacks and test the **effectiveness of their EDR solutions** 【94†source】.

2. Enhancing Physical Security with a Security-First Culture

- **Leadership and Infrastructure Management**: Strong leadership ensures that **physical security measures**, such as **biometric access controls** for data centers, are prioritized alongside **technical defenses**. **Google** exemplifies this balance through its **BeyondCorp model**, where physical and **digital access controls** are aligned to protect sensitive data 【95†source】.

3. Adaptive Policies for Dynamic Threats

- **Using AI for Continuous Monitoring**: AI-powered **UEBA** and **SOAR platforms** provide continuous monitoring of user behavior, much like analyzing a soccer game in real-time to adjust tactics. This ensures that **anomalous activities** are detected early and **automated responses** are triggered to mitigate risks.

Case Study: Integrating the Four Elements at a Large University

The Challenge: A **large university** with **40,000 students** and **5,000 staff members** faced challenges securing access to **research data** and **student records** as it transitioned to **remote learning** during the **COVID-19 pandemic.** The university's **open network** made it vulnerable to **phishing attacks** and **unauthorized access** to research databases.

The Solution: The university adopted a **Zero Trust model** that integrated **technical, tactical, physical,** and **psychological** elements:

- **Technical:** Deployed **AI-driven EDR** to monitor endpoints for **fileless malware** and **phishing attempts** targeting staff. Implemented **MFA** to secure access to research data.

- **Tactical:** Conducted **Red Team exercises** to simulate targeted attacks against **cloud-based learning platforms.** These exercises revealed weaknesses in **access control policies,** leading to improved **adaptive access controls.**

- **Physical:** Enhanced **physical security** at on-campus **data centers** using **biometric access controls** and **video surveillance** to prevent unauthorized entry. This protected **research servers** that stored **sensitive medical data.**

- **Psychological:** Launched a **cybersecurity awareness campaign** among students and staff, emphasizing the importance of **vigilance** in detecting phishing attempts. Leadership held regular **town hall meetings** to discuss emerging threats and gather feedback on **security policies.**

Outcome: By integrating these elements, the university achieved a **30% reduction in phishing incidents** and **improved compliance** with **FERPA** (Family Educational Rights and Privacy Act) and **HIPAA**

regulations   for   **student**   **and**   **medical**
data 【94†source】 【95†source】 . The **security-first mindset**
fostered among staff and students played a crucial role in maintaining a
resilient Zero Trust environment throughout the pandemic.

Conclusion

This chapter illustrates how the **soccer analogy** can help
organizations understand and apply **Zero Trust principles** effectively.
By focusing on **technical tools, strategic adaptations, physical
security,** and **leadership-driven culture**, organizations can build a
balanced Zero Trust strategy that addresses **modern cybersecurity
challenges.** The **university case study** demonstrates the importance
of integrating these elements to achieve a **holistic defense** against
cyber threats.

As we move to the next chapter, we will explore the challenges of
scaling Zero Trust principles in **global enterprises** and how to
maintain **security** while fostering **innovation** in **diverse industries.**

Challenges and Pitfalls in Implementing Zero Trust

- Common Obstacles in Adopting Zero Trust Architectures
- Balancing User Experience with Security
- Addressing Legacy Systems and Network Segmentation Challenges
- Overcoming Resistance to Change in Organizational Culture

Introduction

Implementing **Zero Trust Architecture (ZTA)** promises to enhance **cybersecurity resilience** by shifting the focus from perimeter-based defenses to **identity-based** and **resource-centric** security. However, the journey toward achieving a **Zero Trust model** is not without its challenges. Just as a soccer team faces obstacles such as **injuries, coordination issues**, and **fatigue**, organizations adopting Zero Trust must navigate **technological, cultural**, and **logistical hurdles**. This chapter explores **common obstacles** in implementing Zero Trust, the difficulty of **balancing user experience with security**, challenges posed by **legacy systems**, and the need to **overcome resistance** to cultural change. Through **real-life examples**, we will understand how these challenges manifest and how some organizations have managed to address them.

Common Obstacles in Adopting Zero Trust Architectures

1. Complexity of Deployment

Implementing a **Zero Trust framework** is often more complex than initially anticipated. It involves a thorough understanding of **existing infrastructure, user behavior, data flows**, and **network architecture**. Organizations must map out all potential **access points, user roles**, and **data assets** to enforce the principle of **least privilege**.

- **Network Visibility**: A significant challenge is achieving **complete visibility** into all endpoints, applications, and user interactions. Without a clear picture of who is accessing what, enforcing **contextual access control** becomes difficult.

- **Integration with Existing Systems**: Many organizations face challenges when trying to integrate **new Zero Trust tools** with **existing security systems** like **SIEMs, firewalls**, and **EDR platforms**. Compatibility issues can slow down deployment and lead to **security gaps** if not addressed properly.

Real-Life Example: U.S. Department of Defense (DoD) Zero Trust Initiative The **U.S. Department of Defense** has been working to implement a **Zero Trust model** as part of its **cybersecurity strategy**. One of the significant challenges they faced was the

complexity of integrating Zero Trust principles across a **massive and diverse IT landscape** involving **cloud environments, on-premises systems,** and **classified networks** 【94†source】 【95†source】 . Their journey highlights how even large organizations with substantial resources can struggle with the **complexity of integration** and the need for a **clear, phased approach.**

2. Managing Costs

Transitioning to a Zero Trust model can be **resource-intensive.** Organizations may need to invest in new **identity and access management (IAM) systems, micro-segmentation tools, AI-driven analytics,** and **continuous monitoring solutions.** While the **long-term benefits** of enhanced security are clear, the **initial financial outlay** can be a deterrent, especially for **small and medium-sized enterprises (SMEs).**

- **Infrastructure Upgrades**: Zero Trust often requires **upgrading network infrastructure** to support **micro-segmentation** and **software-defined perimeters** (SDPs), which can be costly.

- **Training Costs**: Employees need to be trained on **new access protocols, MFA procedures,** and **security best practices,** adding to the overall cost of transition.

Real-Life Example: Healthcare Sector In the **healthcare industry,** organizations like **hospitals** and **medical research facilities** face challenges with the **costs of Zero Trust**. Many healthcare institutions operate on **tight budgets** and find it difficult to justify **upgrading**

legacy systems and investing in **new IAM solutions** 【94†source】 . However, the **risk of data breaches** involving patient records and the cost of compliance with regulations like **HIPAA** have driven some to make the necessary investments despite financial constraints.

Balancing User Experience with Security

1. User Friction with Multi-Factor Authentication (MFA)

While **MFA** is a cornerstone of Zero Trust, requiring **multiple authentication steps** can introduce **friction** for users. For example, if employees must use MFA each time they access different applications, it can slow down their workflow, leading to **frustration** and potentially **reduced productivity**.

- **Balancing Security and Convenience**: Organizations need to strike a balance between **robust security measures** and a **smooth user experience**. Using **adaptive MFA**—which only prompts additional authentication when a user's behavior is unusual—can help reduce friction.

- **Usability Testing**: Testing security measures with real users before deploying them organization-wide is critical. This helps identify potential **bottlenecks** and **user experience issues** that can be addressed through **UI improvements**.

Real-Life Example: Dropbox's MFA Rollout Dropbox faced challenges when rolling out **MFA** to its global user base as part of its **Zero Trust initiative**. Users initially resisted the extra steps involved in accessing their accounts. Dropbox addressed this by implementing **risk-based MFA**, where users were only prompted for additional verification if they attempted to access data from **unusual locations** 【95†source】 . This approach helped maintain **high security** while reducing user complaints about the **access process**.

2. Maintaining Performance and Speed

ZTNA can introduce **latency** due to **continuous authentication** and **dynamic access checks**. This can be especially problematic for **remote workers** or **international teams** who rely on **cloud applications** and need **consistent access speeds**.

- **Optimizing Access Policies**: Using **AI-driven solutions** like **User and Entity Behavior Analytics (UEBA)** can help optimize access policies, ensuring that **low-risk users** are granted access without unnecessary delays.

- **Distributed Access Points**: Implementing **distributed cloud access points** can reduce **latency** by **localizing authentication** processes. This ensures that remote users do not experience **significant lag** when accessing corporate resources.

Real-Life Example: Financial Services Firm A **global financial services company** faced **performance issues** after implementing **ZTNA** due to **authentication delays** for remote workers in different regions. By deploying **cloud access security brokers (CASBs)** and **local identity providers**, the company was able to **reduce latency** and ensure that **authentication processes** did not disrupt user productivity 【94†source】 .

Addressing Legacy Systems and Network Segmentation Challenges

1. Legacy System Compatibility

Many organizations rely on **legacy systems** that were designed for **traditional perimeter-based security models**. These systems often lack the **APIs** and **integration capabilities** needed to support **modern Zero Trust tools**, creating **compatibility challenges**.

- **Retrofitting Old Systems**: Retrofitting older systems to support **Zero Trust policies** can be time-consuming and expensive. Organizations may need to use **API gateways** or **proxy servers** to bridge the gap between **legacy applications** and **new security tools**.

- **Gradual Migration Strategy**: Adopting a **phased approach** to Zero Trust—starting with critical applications and gradually extending policies to **legacy systems**—can help manage compatibility issues without disrupting daily operations.

Real-Life Example: Retail Industry A **large retail chain** faced challenges integrating **Zero Trust principles** with its **point-of-sale (POS) systems**, which relied on **outdated software**. By deploying **micro-segmentation** and **secure access gateways** for its POS network, the company was able to **isolate vulnerabilities** and gradually replace outdated systems without compromising the **security of**

customer data 【95†source】 .

2. Network Segmentation Challenges

Micro-segmentation is essential for minimizing **lateral movement** in a **Zero Trust environment**, but implementing it can be challenging, especially in **complex networks**.

- **Over-Segmentation Risks**: Over-segmenting the network can create **management overhead** and **complexity** that slows down operations. Finding the right balance between **segmentation and operational efficiency** is critical.

- **Visibility Gaps**: Without **clear visibility** into all network segments, organizations may find it difficult to identify which assets need to be isolated. Tools like **software-defined networking (SDN)** can provide **better control** and **automation** for **network segmentation**.

Real-Life Example: Energy Sector An **energy company** implementing **Zero Trust** faced challenges with **segmenting its industrial control systems (ICS)** from **corporate IT networks**. Using **SDN solutions**, the company was able to **automate network segmentation** and create isolated zones for **critical infrastructure**, significantly reducing the risk of **cyberattacks** spreading from corporate networks to **operational technology (OT)** systems 【94†source】 .

Overcoming Resistance to Change in Organizational Culture

1. Resistance from Leadership and Employees

A successful **Zero Trust implementation** requires a **cultural shift** where **security becomes a priority** at all levels of the organization. However, **resistance to change** is a common obstacle, especially when employees perceive **new security measures** as **disruptive**.

- **Leadership Advocacy:** Having **executive sponsors** who actively support Zero Trust helps convey the importance of the initiative to the entire organization. Leaders who communicate how Zero Trust aligns with the organization's broader **strategic goals** can help overcome resistance from different departments.

- **Employee Engagement:** Regular **training sessions, town halls,** and **feedback mechanisms** can help employees understand why **Zero Trust policies** are being implemented and how they contribute to **overall security**. Creating a sense of **shared responsibility** for security can also empower employees to take an active role in protecting their organization's digital assets.

Real-Life Example: University Transitioning to Zero Trust A **large public university** faced resistance from faculty when transitioning to **Zero Trust policies** that restricted **data access** based on **user roles**. The university's **IT leadership** conducted **awareness sessions** and worked closely with **faculty committees** to demonstrate the value of **data security** in protecting **student records** and **research**

data. By involving faculty in the **policy development process** and showing them how Zero Trust would directly benefit their work, the university managed to reduce pushback and foster a **collaborative culture** 【94†source】 【95†source】 .

2. Addressing Misconceptions about Zero Trust

Many employees and leaders assume that **Zero Trust** means **zero access** or that it will **hinder productivity**. These misconceptions can be barriers to successful adoption.

- **Clarifying Zero Trust Principles**: Organizations need to emphasize that **Zero Trust** is about **continuous verification** rather than denying access altogether. It ensures that users can **securely access** what they need without exposing the network to unnecessary risks.

- **Highlighting Success Stories**: Sharing examples of **successful Zero Trust implementations** can help overcome doubts. For instance, showcasing how **financial institutions** or **tech companies** have used Zero Trust to protect **sensitive data** while maintaining a **productive workflow** can demonstrate its practical benefits.

Real-Life Example: A Major Healthcare System A **healthcare system** struggled with the perception that Zero Trust would **slow down access** to **patient records** for doctors and nurses. To address this, the IT team ran a **pilot program** in one department, demonstrating that **ZTNA** could actually **streamline access** by eliminating the need for a **VPN** while still meeting **HIPAA**

compliance requirements 【95†source】 . The pilot's success helped **dispel myths** about Zero Trust and encouraged broader adoption across the organization.

Conclusion

Implementing **Zero Trust** is a complex journey that requires addressing **technical challenges, user experience issues, legacy system compatibility,** and **cultural resistance**. Each obstacle is an opportunity for **learning and adaptation,** much like the challenges faced by a soccer team. The examples in this chapter illustrate how organizations across different sectors have navigated these challenges, ultimately building a **resilient cybersecurity posture**. By understanding these common pitfalls and learning from real-world experiences, readers can develop strategies to **overcome obstacles** and successfully implement **Zero Trust** in their own environments.

As we move forward, the next chapter will explore how to **measure the success** of Zero Trust implementations, providing a framework for **continuous improvement** and **long-term resilience** in an evolving **cyber threat landscape.**

10 Future Trends in Zero Trust and Cybersecurity

- The Role of AI and Machine Learning in Future Cybersecurity
- Zero Trust in a World of Increasingly Complex Threats
- The Impact of Regulations and Compliance on Zero Trust Strategies
- Preparing for the Next Generation of Cybersecurity Challenges

Introduction

As the digital landscape continues to evolve, cybersecurity faces a dynamic array of challenges, driven by technological advancements, emerging threats, and regulatory changes. The Zero Trust Architecture (ZTA) has emerged as a cornerstone strategy, prioritizing the principles of "Never Trust, Always Verify" to secure data, networks, and applications. However, the future of Zero Trust is influenced by trends like the integration of AI and machine learning, adaptation to increasingly complex threats, evolving regulations, and the preparations needed for next-generation cybersecurity challenges. This chapter explores these trends, illustrating their implications with real-world examples and insights into how Zero Trust will shape the future of digital security.

The Role of AI and Machine Learning in Future Cybersecurity

1. **AI-Enhanced Threat Detection and Response** As cyber threats become more sophisticated, AI and machine learning (ML) are essential for improving threat detection and incident response. Within a Zero Trust framework, AI tools can analyze vast amounts of network traffic, user behavior, and device data to identify potential anomalies in real-time.

   o **Real-Time Analysis**: AI models detect suspicious activity patterns, such as unusual login attempts or data exfiltration, that might indicate a compromised account or malware presence. This enables immediate actions like isolating affected devices or blocking unauthorized access.

   o **Automated Incident Response**: AI-driven Security Orchestration, Automation, and Response (SOAR) platforms empower organizations to automate responses to threats, such as quarantining compromised accounts or revoking access tokens without human intervention.

Real-Life Example: Darktrace's Self-Learning AI Darktrace, a leader in using self-learning AI for cyber defense, showcased its capabilities during a 2020 cyberattack on a global manufacturer. Darktrace's AI detected unusual data patterns that indicated an early-stage ransomware infection. By analyzing network behavior, the AI enabled the security team to isolate the threat, preventing widespread damage. This example highlights how AI enhances Zero Trust by providing real-time detection and automated responses to complex threats.

2. **Predictive Analytics and Proactive Defense** Predictive analytics allows organizations to anticipate threats before they occur, enabling a proactive security posture. AI models analyze historical attack data and global threat intelligence to predict likely attack vectors and adjust Zero Trust policies.

    o **Risk-Based Authentication**: AI can assign risk scores to users and devices based on factors like login behavior, location, and past activity. Users with higher risk scores may face stricter verification processes, such as additional multi-factor authentication (MFA).

    o **Adaptive Threat Models**: AI integrates with Zero Trust Network Access (ZTNA) to continuously adjust access levels based on real-time threat assessments, ensuring that even trusted users are re-evaluated when their behavior deviates from the norm.

Real-Life Example: CrowdStrike's Predictive Capabilities CrowdStrike's Falcon platform uses machine learning models to analyze billions of events across client networks, helping to identify potential threats before they can cause harm. During the SolarWinds cyberattack in 2020, CrowdStrike's AI-based analytics helped detect anomalous activities linked to the attack, providing early warnings that mitigated its impact. This showcases the importance of predictive analytics in supporting Zero Trust by continuously adapting to evolving threats.

Importance in Zero Trust: The NIST Zero Trust framework emphasizes continuous monitoring and adaptive access control. AI and machine learning are crucial for enhancing detection capabilities and enabling dynamic responses, making Zero Trust environments more effective at preventing breaches and unauthorized access.

Zero Trust in a World of Increasingly Complex Threats

1. **Adapting to Ransomware and Supply Chain Attacks**
   Ransomware and supply chain attacks have become major threats, often bypassing traditional defenses. Zero Trust helps contain these threats by focusing on micro-segmentation and identity verification.

   o **Micro-Segmentation**: By dividing the network into smaller segments, organizations can limit the spread of ransomware and restrict unauthorized access. For instance, a financial institution might segment its payment processing systems from customer records, ensuring that a breach in one system does not compromise others.

   o **Protecting Software Supply Chains**: Zero Trust principles apply to the software development lifecycle, ensuring that code repositories and third-party libraries are subject to strict access controls and continuous validation, reducing the risk of malicious code infiltrating the software supply chain.

Real-Life Example: Colonial Pipeline Ransomware Attack (2021)
The Colonial Pipeline ransomware attack exposed vulnerabilities in critical infrastructure, leading to significant fuel supply disruptions in the eastern United States. A Zero Trust approach could have

minimized the damage by using identity verification for remote access and network segmentation to prevent the ransomware from spreading beyond the initial breach point.

2. **Addressing Insider Threats** Insider threats—such as employees or contractors misusing their access—remain one of the most challenging aspects of cybersecurity. Zero Trust's continuous verification ensures that internal users receive the same scrutiny as external threats.

   o **Least Privilege Access**: Enforcing least privilege means users can only access resources necessary for their role, minimizing the potential damage from compromised credentials.

   o **Behavioral Analytics**: AI-driven behavioral monitoring can detect deviations from normal activities, such as large data downloads or attempts to access restricted files, enabling early detection of insider threats.

Real-Life Example: Tesla Insider Sabotage Attempt (2020)
In 2020, a Tesla employee was approached by a cybercriminal offering a bribe to install malware on Tesla's network. Tesla's Zero Trust framework and internal monitoring tools detected suspicious activity, allowing the company to intervene before significant damage occurred. This demonstrates the importance of continuous verification in mitigating insider risks.

The Impact of Regulations and Compliance on Zero Trust Strategies

1. **Adapting to New Data Privacy Regulations** With a growing

focus on data privacy, regulations like GDPR in the European Union and CCPA in the United States demand stringent data protection measures. Zero Trust helps organizations comply with these regulations through fine-grained access controls and encryption.

- o **Encryption for Compliance**: Zero Trust emphasizes end-to-end encryption, ensuring that personal data remains secure during transmission and storage, aligning with GDPR requirements.
- o **Auditing and Logging**: Detailed access logs allow organizations to demonstrate compliance by showing who accessed sensitive data, when, and why.

Real-Life Example: GDPR Compliance in Financial Services
A European bank implemented a Zero Trust approach to comply with GDPR by using role-based access controls (RBAC) and MFA for accessing customer data. This allowed the bank to limit access to sensitive information and generate audit reports for regulatory reviews.

2. **Government Mandates for Zero Trust Adoption** Governments worldwide are advocating for Zero Trust principles to protect critical infrastructure. In the U.S., the 2021 Executive Order on Improving the Nation's Cybersecurity directed federal agencies to adopt Zero Trust strategies, influencing the private sector as well.

- o **Mandated Multi-Factor Authentication**: Federal mandates require MFA and encryption across systems, aligning with Zero Trust's continuous verification.
- o **NIST Guidelines**: NIST Special Publication 800-207

provides a framework for implementing Zero Trust, helping organizations align their security strategies with federal standards.

Real-Life Example: U.S. Department of Defense's Zero Trust Initiative

The U.S. Department of Defense (DoD) has adopted a Zero Trust framework that includes micro-segmentation, continuous monitoring, and AI-based threat detection to protect national security assets. This large-scale adoption sets an example for other organizations, demonstrating how Zero Trust can be applied in complex environments.

Preparing for the Next Generation of Cybersecurity Challenges

1. **Scaling Zero Trust Across Hybrid and Multi-Cloud Environments** As organizations adopt hybrid and multi-cloud infrastructures, implementing Zero Trust across diverse environments presents new challenges.

   o **Cloud-Native Solutions**: Organizations use cloud-native Zero Trust solutions like ZTNA to manage identity and access control across AWS, Azure, and Google Cloud.

   o **Unified Security Posture**: Identity federation and single sign-on (SSO) help verify user identities consistently across environments, allowing secure access to cloud applications.

Real-Life Example: Netflix's Multi-Cloud Zero Trust Approach

Netflix uses Zero Trust strategies across its cloud platforms, leveraging

AWS IAM and Google Cloud Identity for access controls. This approach ensures secure, authenticated access for its global streaming services, even as the company scales.

2. **The Rise of Quantum Computing and Post-Quantum Cryptography** Quantum computing presents future challenges that could render traditional encryption methods vulnerable. Zero Trust must evolve to include quantum-resistant algorithms.

   o **Post-Quantum Cryptography**: As quantum technology advances, organizations must implement encryption algorithms that are resistant to quantum decryption.

   o **Quantum-Safe Key Management**: Zero Trust systems will need secure key exchanges that remain safe in the face of quantum computing advances.

Real-Life Example: Google's Quantum-Resistant Initiatives Google has experimented with post-quantum cryptography as part of its Zero Trust strategy, testing quantum-resistant algorithms to secure Google Cloud data. This work highlights the importance of preparing for the potential impact of quantum computing.

Conclusion

The future of Zero Trust is shaped by AI advancements, emerging threats, and regulatory shifts. AI and predictive analytics are crucial for real-time threat detection, while post-quantum cryptography prepares organizations for potential future challenges. By understanding these trends, organizations can build resilient Zero Trust architectures that adapt to the evolving cybersecurity landscape. As businesses continue to refine their Zero Trust strategies, staying ahead of these trends will be vital for ensuring long-term security in an ever-changing digital world.

11 Practical Guidelines and Challenges in Zero Trust Implementation

- Understanding the Shift to Zero Trust
- Limitations of Traditional Security Models
- Why Zero Trust is Necessary in Modern Cybersecurity
- Key Components of a Zero Trust Architecture
- Implementation Challenges

Introduction

As the cybersecurity landscape becomes more complex, the **Zero Trust Architecture (ZTA)** framework has emerged as a crucial model to secure modern networks. Developed in response to the limitations of traditional perimeter-based security, Zero Trust requires a shift in how organizations think about **identity, access control, and network security**. This chapter explores the practical steps for implementing Zero Trust, outlines the challenges faced during this transition, and highlights real-world applications based on the **NIST Zero Trust Architecture (ZTA) guidelines**. By focusing on practical insights, this chapter provides actionable guidance for those looking to adopt a Zero Trust model within their organizations.

1. Understanding the Shift to Zero Trust

Limitations of Traditional Security Models

Traditional security models operate on the assumption that networks have a well-defined perimeter, with **firewalls** and **gateways** providing a secure boundary. Once inside, users and devices are often trusted by default. This approach is analogous to a castle with strong walls, where anyone inside the walls is considered safe. However, this model struggles with several issues:

- **Insider Threats**: Once a bad actor gains access inside the network, they can often move laterally with minimal restrictions.

- **Remote Work and Cloud Services**: With the rise of remote work, **cloud services**, and **mobile devices**, the perimeter is no longer clearly defined, making traditional models inadequate for modern cybersecurity challenges.

Why Zero Trust is Necessary in Modern Cybersecurity

Zero Trust shifts the focus from perimeter security to **resource-centric security**. It emphasizes the mantra of **"Never Trust, Always Verify"**, meaning every request—whether from inside or outside the network—must be authenticated and authorized before access is granted. This shift ensures that access is based on **identity verification**, **device health**, and **contextual risk assessments**, making networks more resilient to both internal and external threats.

2. Key Components of a Zero Trust Architecture

Policy Engines, ICAM, and Policy Enforcement Points

Zero Trust relies on several critical components to ensure that access decisions are dynamic and based on real-time data:

- **Policy Engine**: Determines whether a user or device should be granted access to a particular resource. It relies on data from **Identity, Credential, and Access Management (ICAM)** systems to validate user identity.

- **Identity, Credential, and Access Management (ICAM)**: Manages user identities, credentials, and attributes, ensuring that each access request is properly authenticated.

- **Policy Enforcement Points (PEPs)**: Act as gatekeepers, enforcing decisions made by the **Policy Engine** by granting or denying access to resources based on the user's identity and context.

Continuous Authentication and Risk-Based Access Control

Continuous authentication verifies user identity throughout a session, ensuring that no user is trusted for prolonged periods without ongoing validation. This is critical in Zero Trust as it helps to detect **anomalous behaviors** during an active session, such as **unusual access patterns** or **location changes**. **Risk-Based Access Control (RBA)** further adjusts access requirements based on factors like location, device type, and the sensitivity of the requested resource.

3. Implementation Challenges

Integrating Zero Trust with Existing Infrastructure

One of the primary challenges in adopting Zero Trust is integrating its principles with existing network infrastructure. Organizations often have legacy systems that were not designed for **fine-grained access control** and continuous monitoring. Transitioning to a Zero Trust model requires:

- **Retrofitting Legacy Systems**: Updating older systems to support **multi-factor authentication (MFA)**, **encryption**, and **identity management**.

- **Hybrid Environments**: Adapting Zero Trust for environments that include **on-premises servers**, **cloud services**, and **remote workforces**, ensuring consistent policies across all access points.

Balancing Usability and Security: Avoiding User Frustration

Implementing **strict authentication** and **verification protocols** can sometimes frustrate users, particularly if it results in **slow login processes** or **access denials**. The challenge is to maintain high security without negatively impacting **user experience**.

- **Adaptive Access Control** helps by adjusting security measures based on real-time risk assessments, reducing friction for trusted users while still enforcing strict checks for high-risk actions.

Addressing Organizational Readiness and Cultural Change

For Zero Trust to be effective, it must be embraced by all levels of an organization, from **executive leadership** to **IT staff**. Often, there is resistance due to a lack of understanding about what Zero Trust entails or fears about the cost and complexity of implementation. To overcome this:

- **Training and Awareness Programs**: Educating stakeholders about the benefits of Zero Trust and how it improves overall security.

- **Incremental Adoption**: Adopting Zero Trust in stages,

starting with the most critical assets and expanding as the organization becomes more comfortable with the approach.

4. Benefits of Zero Trust

Enhanced Flexibility for Remote Work

With **remote work** and **cloud-based applications** becoming the norm, Zero Trust enables secure access without relying on traditional **VPNs**. This allows employees to access resources securely from anywhere without sacrificing productivity.

Improved Defense Against Insider Threats

Zero Trust assumes that users inside the network can be as dangerous as those outside, making it ideal for combating **insider threats**. Every user's access is limited to only what they need, and behavior is continuously monitored for **anomalies**.

Limiting Breach Impact Through Micro-Segmentation

By dividing networks into **micro-segments**, Zero Trust restricts the movement of an attacker even if they compromise part of the network. This prevents **lateral movement**, minimizing the impact of potential breaches.

5. Real-World Case Studies

Examples from Industry Collaborations (e.g., AWS, Microsoft)

Leading technology companies like **AWS**, **Microsoft**, and **Google** have partnered with NIST to develop adaptable Zero Trust solutions. For example:

- **AWS Zero Trust Solutions**: Integrates **identity management** with **cloud-native security** to ensure that each access request is continuously verified, even within cloud environments.

- **Microsoft's Zero Trust Strategy**: Emphasizes **multi-factor authentication, conditional access,** and **risk-based policies,** making it easier for enterprises to secure their **Azure environments.**

How Federal Agencies Adapted Zero Trust Principles

Following the **2021 Executive Order on Improving the Nation's Cybersecurity,** U.S. federal agencies were required to adopt Zero Trust architectures. This led to initiatives like:

- **Adoption of MFA across all government systems** to reduce the risks of credential theft.

- **Continuous monitoring of access patterns** to identify and respond to suspicious behavior in real-time.

6. NIST's Role in Standardizing Zero Trust

Summary of NIST Special Publication 800-207

NIST's Special Publication 800-207 defines the principles and components of a Zero Trust Architecture. It serves as a foundational guide for both public and private organizations in implementing Zero Trust. Key aspects include:

- **Access Control Policies**: Guidelines for using ICAM systems to validate every access request.

- **Policy Decision Points (PDPs)** and **Policy Enforcement Points (PEPs)**: Ensuring that decisions about access are made based on **real-time data** about users and devices.

Key Takeaways from the NIST Fact Sheet

The fact sheet emphasizes that implementing Zero Trust is a journey that requires **planning, adaptation, and a willingness to rethink traditional approaches** to security. It also highlights that Zero Trust is not a one-size-fits-all solution, but rather a framework that needs to be tailored to an organization's specific needs and environment.

Conclusion

The **Zero Trust Architecture** represents a fundamental shift in how organizations approach cybersecurity. By leveraging insights from **NIST guidelines**, focusing on **continuous authentication**, and addressing the challenges of implementation, organizations can build a robust Zero Trust framework that adapts to the complexities of modern threats. As we continue to face new challenges in cybersecurity, Zero Trust offers a pathway to **greater resilience, flexibility, and security**. This chapter provides a roadmap for organizations looking to adopt Zero Trust, ensuring they are prepared for the evolving cyber threat landscape.

- Reflections on the Soccer Analogy and Cybersecurity
- Key Takeaways for Cybersecurity Leaders and Practitioners
- Continuous Learning and Adapting to New Threats

Chapter 11 - Conclusion: The Power of Strategy, Resilience, and Adaptability

Introduction

The journey through **Zero Trust Architecture (ZTA)** has revealed a complex yet powerful approach to **cybersecurity** that is as strategic and dynamic as a game of soccer. Like a well-coached team, organizations must adapt their **defenses**, anticipate **attacks**, and stay **resilient** in the face of evolving threats. Throughout this book, the analogy of soccer has served as a guiding framework to understand the **technical**, **tactical**, **physical**, and **psychological** elements that contribute to a successful **Zero Trust implementation**. In this final chapter, we reflect on the **soccer analogy**, summarize the **key lessons** for **cybersecurity leaders**, and emphasize the importance of **continuous learning** in an ever-changing threat landscape.

Reflections on the Soccer Analogy and Cybersecurity

1. A Strategic Approach to Defense

In soccer, a well-rounded defense involves not just individual skills but also **strategic coordination** among players. Similarly, **Zero Trust** demands a strategic alignment of **technical tools, policies**, and **leadership** to create a **holistic cybersecurity posture**. The soccer analogy helped us understand how **technical skills** like **Endpoint Detection and Response (EDR), encryption**, and **Identity and Access Management (IAM)** provide the foundational defense, much like a goalie and defenders protect the net.

- **Coordination Across Teams**: Just as a soccer coach adjusts the strategy based on the opponent, **cybersecurity teams** must constantly adapt their **Zero Trust strategies** to address new threats and adjust **policies** as risks evolve. For example, **Google's BeyondCorp** framework emphasized the importance of **identity-based access** over traditional network perimeters, much like a coach transitioning from a defensive to an offensive strategy based on the flow of the game.

2. The Importance of Adaptability and Resilience

Adaptability is crucial in both soccer and cybersecurity. A soccer player must adjust to the movement of the ball and the positioning of opponents, just as an organization must adapt to **new attack vectors** and **regulatory changes. Zero Trust** is inherently **adaptive**, requiring continuous validation of **user identities, device health**, and **network conditions**.

- **Real-Time Responses**: The concept of **continuous**

monitoring and **automated responses** in Zero Trust mirrors the way a soccer team adapts in real-time during a match. For instance, **AI-driven threat detection** tools like **Darktrace** can identify suspicious activities as they occur and take **immediate actions,** such as isolating compromised devices. This real-time adaptability is essential for maintaining a **resilient cybersecurity posture.**

3. A Long-Term Commitment to Security

Just as a soccer team trains rigorously and builds a **winning culture,** successful **Zero Trust implementation** requires **long-term commitment** from **leadership** and **staff.** It is not just about deploying tools; it is about fostering a **security-first culture** that prioritizes **continuous learning** and **awareness.**

- **Building a Culture of Security**: Organizations like **Tesla,** which thwarted an insider threat attempt in 2020, have shown how a **culture of vigilance** can help detect and prevent internal risks. In the same way that a soccer team's mindset can determine its success, an organization's **attitude towards security** influences how well it can respond to cyber threats.

Key Takeaways for Cybersecurity Leaders and Practitioners

1. Embrace the Principle of "Never Trust, Always Verify"

At the core of **Zero Trust** is the idea that **no user or device** should be trusted by default, even if they are inside the network. This mindset shift is fundamental for creating a **defense-in-depth strategy** that aligns with the **NIST Zero Trust framework.**

- **Actionable Advice:** Leaders should ensure that **identity**

verification and **multi-factor authentication (MFA)** are enforced for every access request, regardless of the user's location or role. This principle helps prevent lateral movement, which is often a common tactic in **sophisticated breaches** like the **SolarWinds attack**.

2. Focus on Continuous Improvement and Monitoring

Cyber threats are constantly evolving, making it critical to **continuously monitor** network activity and **adapt security policies** based on **real-time insights**. The focus should be on **detecting anomalies** and **automating responses** to minimize the time between detection and action.

- **Actionable Advice**: Implementing tools like **User and Entity Behavior Analytics (UEBA)** can help identify unusual behavior patterns that may indicate a potential **insider threat** or **account compromise**. This is especially relevant for industries like **healthcare** and **finance**, where real-time data access is critical for business operations.

3. Integrate AI and Automation to Stay Ahead of Threats

As **AI and machine learning** become more sophisticated, they will play an increasingly crucial role in **enhancing Zero Trust capabilities**. AI can help predict **potential threats, adjust access controls dynamically**, and **automate incident responses** to reduce the workload on **cybersecurity teams**.

- **Actionable Advice**: Organizations should explore integrating **AI-driven security platforms** like **CrowdStrike** and **Darktrace** to complement their **Zero Trust framework**. These platforms provide **predictive analytics** and **automated threat**

hunting, helping organizations to **identify vulnerabilities** before they can be exploited.

Continuous Learning and Adapting to New Threats

1. The Importance of Ongoing Training and Awareness

In the rapidly changing world of **cybersecurity**, staying informed about **new attack methods** and **emerging technologies** is essential. Just as a soccer team reviews its **performance** and **adjusts training** based on each match, **cybersecurity practitioners** must engage in **continuous learning** to remain effective.

- **Regular Training**: Organizations should conduct **regular training sessions** for employees, focusing on **recognizing phishing attempts**, **secure handling of data**, and the importance of **multi-factor authentication**. This not only helps in **preventing human errors** but also reinforces a **security-first culture** across the organization.

2. Adapting to Technological Advances

New technologies like **quantum computing** and **5G networks** will reshape the **cybersecurity landscape**, presenting both **opportunities** and **challenges**. It is critical for **cybersecurity leaders** to stay updated on these trends and **prepare their Zero Trust strategies** to remain relevant.

- **Investing in Research**: Organizations should invest in **research and development** to understand how **post-quantum cryptography** can protect their **data** as **quantum computing** advances. Staying ahead of such trends ensures that **security architectures** remain robust against **future threats**.

3. Building Partnerships and Collaborations

In soccer, a strong **team dynamic** is essential for success. Similarly, **collaboration** with **industry peers, regulatory bodies**, and **cybersecurity forums** is key to staying updated on **best practices** and **emerging threats**.

- **Leveraging Industry Knowledge**: Cybersecurity practitioners can benefit from **sharing threat intelligence** and **learning from incidents** that have impacted similar organizations. This knowledge sharing helps create a more **resilient cybersecurity community** and ensures that **Zero Trust strategies** evolve in line with **industry standards**.

Conclusion

The journey toward **Zero Trust** is not a one-time effort but a **continuous process** of **learning, adapting**, and **strategizing**. Just as a soccer team evolves its **game plan** with each new opponent, organizations must refine their **Zero Trust strategies** to address the **cyber threats** of tomorrow. By embracing the principles of **"Never Trust, Always Verify"**, focusing on **continuous improvement**, and leveraging the power of **AI and automation**, organizations can build a **resilient security posture** that stands the test of time.

As students and practitioners move forward in their **cybersecurity careers**, the lessons from this book will serve as a **playbook**—not just for understanding **Zero Trust**, but for developing the **strategic mindset** necessary to navigate the **complex cyber threat landscape**. The **soccer analogy** provides a lens through which we can view the **discipline, teamwork**, and **adaptability** that define successful

cybersecurity practices. The ultimate goal is to build a **secure and adaptive digital environment**, where **every access point** is continuously monitored, every **vulnerability** is anticipated, and every **user interaction** is subject to **rigorous verification**.

Glossary of Key Terms in Zero Trust and Cybersecurity

A

1. **Access Control**: A security technique that regulates who or what can access resources in a computing environment. Zero Trust applies granular access control, ensuring users have only the permissions they need.
   Example: Role-Based Access Control (RBAC) is used in AWS Identity and Access Management (IAM) to limit access based on a user's role within the company.

2. **Adaptive Access Control**: A dynamic form of access control that adjusts permissions based on user behavior, location, and device health.
   Example: Google's BeyondCorp uses adaptive access to change access levels if a user logs in from an unfamiliar location.

3. **AI in Cybersecurity**: Artificial intelligence methods used to analyze security data, identify anomalies, and automate incident response. AI enhances Zero Trust through continuous monitoring and predictive analytics.

Example: Darktrace uses AI to detect deviations in network behavior in real-time.

4. **Authentication**: The process of verifying the identity of a user or device before granting access.
   Example: Using biometrics like fingerprints or facial recognition to log into a secure device.

B

5. **Behavioral Analytics**: Analyzing user behavior patterns to detect anomalies that might indicate suspicious activities. This supports Zero Trust by identifying compromised accounts.
   Example: Splunk uses User and Entity Behavior Analytics (UEBA) to identify abnormal login activities, such as accessing data from multiple locations within a short period.

6. **Biometric Authentication**: Using physical traits such as fingerprints or facial recognition to verify identity.
   Example: Apple Face ID uses facial recognition for secure access to devices.

7. **Business Impact Analysis (BIA)**: Identifies critical business functions and assesses the potential impact of a disruption on operations.
   Example: A hospital conducts a BIA to determine the impact of a DDoS attack on patient care systems.

8. **BYOD (Bring Your Own Device) Security**: Policies that ensure the secure use of personal devices within a corporate network.

Example: Requiring encryption and remote wipe capabilities for smartphones accessing company data.

C

9. **Capital One Case Study**: A real-world example of how AI and machine learning were used to detect and mitigate cyber threats in a financial services environment.

10. **CIA Triad (Confidentiality, Integrity, Availability)**: A fundamental model in cybersecurity focused on three key principles to ensure data is protected, unaltered, and accessible. *Example*: Implementing encryption protects confidentiality, while backups ensure data availability.

11. **CISA (Cybersecurity and Infrastructure Security Agency)**: A U.S. government agency responsible for improving cybersecurity across federal agencies and protecting critical infrastructure. *Example*: CISA's Zero Trust Maturity Model guides federal agencies in implementing Zero Trust.

12. **Cloud Access Security Broker (CASB)**: Monitors cloud service usage and enforces security policies. *Example*: Microsoft Cloud App Security acts as a CASB to manage access and secure data across cloud platforms.

13. **Cloud Security**: Measures to protect data and applications stored in the cloud from cyber threats. *Example*: AWS provides tools like Identity and Access Management (IAM) to control user access to cloud resources.

14. **Continuous Monitoring**: Ongoing surveillance of networks and systems to detect and respond to threats.
Example: Using Splunk for continuous monitoring of logs and network traffic.

15. **CrowdStrike**: A cybersecurity company specializing in endpoint detection and response (EDR) solutions.
Example: CrowdStrike's Falcon platform detects and responds to endpoint threats.

16. **Cybersecurity**: The practice of protecting networks, systems, applications, and data from cyberattacks and unauthorized access.
Example: A bank uses encryption and multi-factor authentication to protect customer data.

17. **Cyber Threats**: Potential malicious activities that aim to disrupt, steal, or damage digital information.
Example: Ransomware encrypting a company's data and demanding payment for decryption.

D

18. **Data Encryption**: Transforming data into a secure format that can only be accessed by those with a decryption key.
Example: Transport Layer Security (TLS) secures communications between web browsers and servers.

19. **Data Privacy**: The protection of personal data from unauthorized access.

Example: GDPR regulations require companies to secure customer data and notify users of any breaches.

20. **Deception Technologies**: Techniques like honeypots that lure attackers, allowing organizations to observe their tactics.
Example: A honeypot is set up to lure attackers targeting IoT devices.

21. **DDoS (Distributed Denial of Service) Attack**: A cyberattack where multiple systems overwhelm a network with traffic, causing a disruption of services.
Example: Cloudflare provides DDoS protection by filtering out malicious traffic.

22. **Digital Security**: Tools and practices used to protect digital assets and personal information from cyber threats.
Example: Using a password manager to store complex passwords securely.

E

23. **EDR (Endpoint Detection and Response)**: Continuously monitors endpoints for threats, providing real-time analysis and response.
Example: SentinelOne detects and mitigates suspicious activities on workstations.

24. **Encryption**: See Data Encryption.

25. **Ethical Hacking**: Authorized testing of systems to find and fix vulnerabilities before malicious hackers can exploit them.

Example: A penetration tester simulates an attack to test a company's defenses.

26. **Equifax Data Breach**: A major data breach that exposed the personal information of millions, highlighting the need for robust cybersecurity.

F

27. **Firewalls**: Devices or software that filter network traffic based on security rules.

    Example: Next-generation firewalls (NGFWs) provide deep packet inspection for enhanced security.

28. **Financial Services Case Study**: Analyzes how financial institutions use Zero Trust to protect sensitive data.

H

29. **Honeypots**: Decoy systems designed to attract and trap attackers, providing insights into their methods.

    Example: A fake server is deployed to observe attacker behavior.

30. **Hybrid Work Models**: Work structures that combine remote and in-office work, requiring secure access methods.

    Example: Using ZTNA to ensure secure connections for remote employees.

I

31. **Identity and Access Management (IAM)**: Manages digital identities and controls user access to resources.

    Example: Okta integrates IAM with MFA for secure access to applications.

32. **Incident Response**: Processes for detecting, managing, and recovering from cybersecurity incidents.

    Example: Isolating infected systems during a ransomware attack.

33. **Information Security**: Protecting information from unauthorized access, alteration, or destruction.

    Example: Using encryption and backups to safeguard patient records.

34. **Insider Threats**: Risks posed by individuals within an organization.

    Example: A disgruntled employee stealing sensitive company data.

35. **IoT Security**: Protecting Internet of Things devices from cyber threats.

    Example: Encrypting data transmissions from smart home devices to ensure security.

L

36. **Least Privilege Principle**: Granting users the minimum access rights needed to perform their roles.

Example: A customer service representative has access to customer records but not financial data.

37. **Leadership Decisions**: Strategic choices made by executives to prioritize cybersecurity.

    Example: A CEO prioritizes Zero Trust adoption across the organization.

38. **Legacy Systems**: Older hardware or software systems that may not be compatible with modern security measures.

    Example: A 20-year-old database system that lacks encryption.

M

39. **Machine Learning**: AI techniques that allow systems to learn from data and improve over time.

    Example: Identifying new phishing patterns using historical attack data.

40. **Marriott Data Breach**: A significant data breach that exposed millions of customers' data, emphasizing the importance of cybersecurity.

41. **Multi-Factor Authentication (MFA)**: Requiring two or more verification factors for access.

    Example: A combination of a password and a fingerprint scan.

N

42. **Network Segmentation**: Dividing a network into smaller parts to reduce potential damage in case of a breach.

    Example: Separating guest Wi-Fi from internal networks.

43. **NIST (National Institute of Standards and Technology)**: Provides standards and guidelines for cybersecurity, including Zero Trust models.

    Example: NIST SP 800-207 offers guidance for implementing Zero Trust Architecture.

P

44. **Penetration Testing**: Simulating attacks to find vulnerabilities in systems.

    Example: A Red Team tests a company's defenses by simulating an external attack.

45. **Phishing**: A social engineering tactic to trick individuals into revealing sensitive information.

    Example: A fake email claims to be from a bank and asks for login credentials.

46. **Policy Development**: Creating policies to govern security practices within an organization.

    Example: Establishing a BYOD policy to regulate personal device use at work.

R

47. **Red Team Exercises**: Simulated attacks by a group to test an organization's defenses.

    Example: A Red Team tests network security by simulating a cyberattack.

48. **Remote Work Security**: Measures to secure employees working outside the office.

    Example: Using a VPN to securely connect remote workers to the corporate network.

49. **Risk-Based Authentication (RBA)**: Adjusting authentication based on the assessed risk level of each access attempt.

    Example: Additional verification when logging in from a new device.

S

50. **SOAR (Security Orchestration, Automation, and Response)**: Platforms that automate security operations, including incident detection and response.

    Example: Automating malware analysis with a SOAR tool like Splunk.

51. **Supply Chain Security**: Ensuring that third-party vendors and tools used in a business's operations are secure.

    Example: Securing third-party software integrations to prevent incidents like the SolarWinds breach.

T

52. **Threat Intelligence**: Collecting and analyzing data about threats to help organizations adjust security measures.
Example: Using threat intelligence feeds to stay informed about the latest phishing attacks.

U

53. **User and Entity Behavior Analytics (UEBA)**: Using AI to monitor user behavior and detect deviations from the norm.
Example: Detecting a user downloading large amounts of data outside regular working hours.

V

54. **Virtual Private Networks (VPNs)**: A tool that encrypts internet connections for secure remote access.
Example: NordVPN provides secure browsing by encrypting data traffic.

Z

55. **Zero Trust**: A security model that requires verification of every request and assumes no implicit trust for any entity.

Example: Requiring identity verification for all access requests, even from internal users.

56. **Zero Trust Architecture (ZTA)**: A framework that applies Zero Trust principles across an organization's entire IT environment.

    Example: Using micro-segmentation and continuous monitoring for all internal network traffic.

57. **Zero-Day Vulnerabilities**: Security flaws that are unknown to the software vendor and have no patch.

    Example: The WannaCry ransomware exploited a zero-day vulnerability in Microsoft Windows.

Chapter 12 - Recommended Reading and Resources for Further Study

Introduction

Building a comprehensive understanding of **Zero Trust Architecture (ZTA)** and **cybersecurity** requires more than just foundational knowledge; it involves continuous learning and exploring the evolving landscape of threats, technologies, and best practices. This chapter provides a curated list of **recommended reading materials, industry resources**, and **academic references** to support further study in the field of Zero Trust and cybersecurity. These resources are particularly valuable for **college sophomores, juniors, seniors, and first-year master's students** who seek to deepen their knowledge beyond the scope of this book.

1. Foundational Documents and Standards

A) NIST Publications

1. **NIST Special Publication 800-207: Zero Trust Architecture**

    o   A definitive guide from the **National Institute of Standards and Technology (NIST)** on Zero Trust. This document outlines the principles, architecture components, and best practices for implementing Zero Trust in various environments. It is the foundational text for understanding ZTA from a standards-based perspective.

    o   *Link*: NIST SP 800-207

2. **NIST Cybersecurity Framework (CSF)**

    o   While not solely focused on Zero Trust, the **NIST CSF** provides a comprehensive framework for managing cybersecurity risk. It is widely used in both the private and public sectors to align security strategies with best practices.

- o   *Link*: NIST Cybersecurity Framework

3.   **NIST Special Publication 800-53: Security and Privacy Controls for Information Systems and Organizations**

- o   This publication details a catalog of security and privacy controls that align with Zero Trust principles. It is essential for organizations seeking to implement a robust set of security measures.

- o   *Link*: NIST SP 800-53

B) Industry Reports and Guides

4.   **"The Forrester Zero Trust Model"**

- o   Forrester Research is credited with originating the concept of Zero Trust. This report outlines the core principles of Zero Trust and provides insights into how organizations can move beyond perimeter-based security.

- o   *Link*: Available through Forrester's research portal, typically accessed through libraries or institutional subscriptions.

5.   **Gartner's Zero Trust Network Access (ZTNA) Hype Cycle Reports**

- o   These reports from **Gartner** offer insights into the maturity and adoption of **Zero Trust Network Access (ZTNA)** technologies, evaluating vendors and technologies based on their market positioning.

- o   *Link*: Available through Gartner's research portal, often accessed through academic or professional subscriptions.

2. Books and Academic Texts

A) Key Books on Zero Trust and Cybersecurity

6. **"Zero Trust Networks: Building Secure Systems in Untrusted Networks" by Evan Gilman and Doug Barth**

    o This book is an excellent resource for a deep dive into building Zero Trust environments, including practical advice on **network segmentation, authentication strategies**, and **access control**. It is particularly suited for students who want a technical understanding of Zero Trust implementation.

    o *ISBN*: 978-1491962190

7. **"Cybersecurity and Cyberwar: What Everyone Needs to Know" by P.W. Singer and Allan Friedman**

    o This book provides a broad overview of **cybersecurity issues**, including discussions of **threats, nation-state actors**, and the evolution of **cyberwarfare**. It is valuable for understanding the global context in which Zero Trust is implemented.

    o *ISBN*: 978-0199918119

8. **"Network Security Through Data Analysis: From Data to Action" by Michael Collins**

    o A valuable resource for those interested in **data analytics** in the context of **network security**. It explores techniques for analyzing **network traffic, identifying anomalies**, and applying these insights in a Zero Trust framework.

    o *ISBN*: 978-1491962824

B) Academic Journals and Articles

9. **IEEE Security & Privacy Magazine**

    o Published by the **IEEE Computer Society**, this journal covers cutting-edge research and case studies on security and privacy, including topics related to **Zero Trust** and **AI-based threat detection**. It is ideal for students seeking peer-reviewed articles and the latest research.

- o *Link*: IEEE Security & Privacy

10. **"The Road to Zero Trust" by John Kindervag** (Article)

- John Kindervag, the creator of the Zero Trust model, offers insights into how organizations can begin their journey toward Zero Trust. This article is a great resource for understanding the practical aspects of Zero Trust adoption.

- *Link*: Available through **Forrester Research** and **industry publications** like **CSO Online**.

3. Online Courses and Certification Programs

A) Online Learning Platforms

11. **Coursera - "Introduction to Cyber Security Specialization" by the University of Maryland**

- This course covers foundational cybersecurity concepts, including **identity management** and **access control**. It is a good starting point for students looking to strengthen their knowledge before diving deeper into Zero Trust.

- *Link*: Coursera Cybersecurity Specialization

12. **edX - "Zero Trust Security" by Microsoft**

- Offered through **edX**, this course focuses specifically on the implementation of **Zero Trust** within enterprise environments, leveraging **Microsoft Azure** tools and services. It includes practical labs and assessments.

- *Link*: edX Zero Trust Security

13. **SANS Institute - SEC401: Security Essentials Bootcamp Style**

- The **SANS Institute** is a leading provider of cybersecurity training. SEC401 covers fundamental concepts, including **network security**, **authentication**, and **incident response**, aligning well with the principles of Zero Trust.

- *Link*: SANS SEC401

4. Community Resources and Cybersecurity Forums

A) Professional Associations and Communities

14. ISACA (Information Systems Audit and Control Association)

- ISACA offers resources on **cybersecurity frameworks**, including **Zero Trust**. Their community forums and events are valuable for networking and discussing best practices.

- *Link*: ISACA Zero Trust Resources

15. OWASP (Open Web Application Security Project)

- OWASP provides a wide range of tools and resources for understanding **application security**, which is integral to Zero Trust. Their guides on secure coding and **API security** can help in building secure application layers.

- *Link*: OWASP

16. CISA's Zero Trust Maturity Model Community Forum

- Hosted by **CISA**, this forum is a place for cybersecurity professionals to share experiences, ask questions, and learn about Zero Trust implementations in **public sector environments**.

- *Link*: CISA Zero Trust Community

Conclusion

These resources and readings provide a path for **continuous learning** and

practical application of **Zero Trust principles**. By exploring the foundational guides from **NIST**, industry reports, academic research, and engaging in **online courses**, students and professionals can stay updated on the latest developments in Zero Trust and **cybersecurity**. This recommended reading list serves as a starting point for those who wish to dive deeper into the **technical, tactical, and strategic elements** of Zero Trust, ensuring a robust understanding of this critical security framework.

Sample Security Policy Templates for Organizations

Introduction

Establishing well-defined **security policies** is fundamental for organizations aiming to protect their **digital infrastructure** and implement **Zero Trust Architecture (ZTA)**. These policies guide how employees, systems, and devices should behave in order to maintain a secure environment, minimize risks, and ensure compliance with **industry regulations**. This chapter provides **detailed security policy templates** for various aspects of **cybersecurity management**, offering a comprehensive guide that organizations can adapt to their needs. Each template includes specific sections, detailed descriptions, and example language to ensure clarity and effectiveness.

1. Acceptable Use Policy (AUP)

Purpose:
The **Acceptable Use Policy (AUP)** defines the appropriate use of an organization's IT resources, including internet usage, email, software applications, and hardware. It ensures users understand their responsibilities when accessing the organization's assets and outlines both **permitted** and **prohibited activities** to prevent misuse.

Example Sections:

- **Scope:**
  This policy applies to all employees, contractors, consultants, and other personnel using the organization's IT resources, regardless of location (on-premises or remote).
  Example: "This policy applies to all personnel using the organization's IT resources, including full-time, part-time employees, interns, contractors, and vendors."

- **Acceptable Uses**:
  Describes activities that are allowed, such as accessing
  company email, using the internet for business research, and
  using **licensed software**.
  Example: "Internet access is provided for business purposes,
  including research, email communication, and accessing
  approved cloud-based tools."

- **Prohibited Activities**:
  Lists activities that are not allowed, such as accessing **illegal
  websites**, sharing **confidential information** on social media,
  or downloading unapproved software.
  Example: "Users are prohibited from accessing adult content,
  gambling websites, or engaging in activities that could harm the
  organization's reputation."

- **Monitoring and Compliance**:
  Details the organization's right to monitor network and device
  usage to ensure compliance.
  Example: "The organization reserves the right to monitor all
  network activity, including email and internet usage, to ensure
  compliance with this policy."

2. Identity and Access Management (IAM) Policy

Purpose:
An **IAM Policy** ensures that **user identities** are verified and that
access to systems and data is based on **the principle of least privilege**.
It outlines procedures for **user authentication, authorization**, and
access control, which are key elements of **Zero Trust Architecture**.

Example Sections:

- **User Account Management**:
  Defines processes for creating, modifying, and deleting user
  accounts. This includes **onboarding, role changes**, and

termination procedures to ensure that access is kept up-to-date.

Example: "New user accounts must be created following the approval of a department head, and access rights must be aligned with job responsibilities."

- **Authentication Requirements**:
  Specifies **Multi-Factor Authentication (MFA)** requirements, **password complexity** rules, and device-based authentication methods to ensure secure access.
  Example: "All users accessing critical systems must use MFA, requiring a combination of a password and a one-time passcode sent via an authenticated device."

- **Access Review and Audit**:
  Requires regular **audits** of user access rights to ensure compliance with the **least privilege** principle. It includes reviewing **inactive accounts** and monitoring **unusual login activities**.
  Example: "Access reviews must be conducted quarterly by the IT department, and any discrepancies should be resolved within 10 business days."

3. Data Encryption Policy

Purpose:
The **Data Encryption Policy** ensures that **sensitive data** is protected through encryption during transmission and storage, maintaining **confidentiality** and **integrity**. This policy specifies encryption standards and methods for **data at rest** (stored data) and **data in transit** (data being transferred over networks).

Example Sections:

- **Scope**:
  Defines what types of data are covered by the encryption

policy, such as **customer data**, **intellectual property**, and **financial information**.

Example: "This policy applies to all sensitive data, including customer payment information, personnel files, and proprietary research data."

- **Encryption Standards**:
  Specifies encryption protocols like **AES-256** for data storage and **TLS 1.2 or higher** for data transmission.
  Example: "All data stored in databases must be encrypted using **AES-256**, and all data transmissions must use **TLS 1.2** or above."

- **Key Management**:
  Outlines procedures for creating, managing, and rotating encryption keys to prevent unauthorized access. It includes using **hardware security modules (HSMs)** for key storage.
  Example: "Encryption keys must be rotated every 90 days, and keys must be stored securely using HSMs."

4. Incident Response Policy

Purpose:
The **Incident Response (IR) Policy** provides a framework for responding to **cybersecurity incidents**, including **data breaches**, **ransomware attacks**, and **phishing attempts**. It ensures that incidents are handled quickly to minimize impact and prevent future occurrences.

Example Sections:

- **Roles and Responsibilities**:
  Defines the roles within the **Incident Response Team (IRT)**, such as **Incident Commander**, **Forensics Specialist**, and **Communications Lead**.
  Example: "The Incident Commander is responsible for

coordinating the response activities and communicating with senior management."

- **Incident Classification:**
  Describes how incidents are classified based on their severity, such as **Low, Medium, High,** and **Critical.**
  Example: "A **Critical** incident involves unauthorized access to customer data, requiring immediate response and regulatory notification."

- **Response Procedures:**
  Details the steps for **containment, eradication,** and **recovery.** This includes isolating affected systems and conducting a forensic analysis to understand the attack vector.
  Example: "In the event of a ransomware attack, affected systems should be disconnected from the network, and backups should be reviewed before initiating recovery."

- **Post-Incident Review:**
  Requires a thorough review after resolving an incident to identify **lessons learned** and improve **response capabilities.**
  Example: "A post-incident review must be conducted within 30 days of resolution, with a report submitted to the **Chief Information Security Officer (CISO).**"

5. Remote Access Policy

Purpose:
A **Remote Access Policy** governs how employees connect to the organization's network when working offsite. It ensures that **remote connections** are secure and comply with **Zero Trust principles,** particularly when accessing **cloud services** or **internal applications.**

Example Sections:

- **Authentication Requirements:**

Requires MFA for all remote access and adherence to **password policies**. It may also include requirements for **device security**, such as using **encrypted laptops**.
Example: "All remote users must authenticate using MFA and must ensure that their devices have the latest security patches."

- **Approved Remote Access Methods**:
  Lists the approved tools and platforms for remote access, such as **VPNs, ZTNA solutions**, or **Virtual Desktop Infrastructure (VDI)**.
  Example: "Remote access must be established using the organization's approved **ZTNA platform** for access to internal applications."

- **Monitoring and Logging**:
  Describes how remote access sessions will be logged and monitored for **anomalous activities**.
  Example: "Remote access logs will be reviewed weekly for any unusual login attempts or access patterns."

6. BYOD (Bring Your Own Device) Policy

Purpose:
The **BYOD Policy** outlines the security requirements for employees using their personal devices to access corporate networks and resources. This policy ensures that personal devices comply with **security standards** to prevent **data breaches**.

Example Sections:

- **Device Registration**:
  Describes the process for registering personal devices with the IT department and obtaining approval for use.
  Example: "All personal devices must be registered with IT before they can be used to access company resources."

- **Security Requirements:**
  Specifies the minimum security settings for personal devices, such as **device encryption, remote wipe capability**, and **anti-malware software**.
  Example: "All personal devices accessing corporate resources must be encrypted and have **anti-malware software** installed."

- **Data Management:**
  Outlines the use of **containerization** or **mobile device management (MDM)** tools to separate personal and business data on employee-owned devices.
  Example: "Corporate email must be accessed through a secure container provided by the MDM solution."

Conclusion

These **sample security policy templates** offer a starting point for developing robust cybersecurity frameworks that align with **Zero Trust principles**. By tailoring these templates to their specific needs, organizations can ensure compliance with **regulatory requirements**, protect **sensitive data**, and maintain a **secure environment**. Adopting these policies will help organizations establish clear guidelines for behavior, access, and incident management, creating a **resilient and adaptable security posture**.

This chapter is designed as a practical tool for **students** and **cybersecurity practitioners**, offering a detailed roadmap for creating policies that meet the demands of today's complex digital landscape. Let me know if you need additional information orThese expanded **sample security policy templates** provide a practical and comprehensive foundation for creating a strong security framework within an organization. The detailed breakdowns include specific sections, purposes, and examples, making it easier for organizations to adapt the templates to their specific needs. They align with **Zero Trust principles** and emphasize **security best practices**, ensuring that policies are both effective and easy to understand. By implementing these policies, organizations can better protect their digital assets, minimize risks, and foster a culture of security awareness. If you need further details or specific customizations, feel free to ask!

National Institute of Standards and Technology (NIST).

- NIST Special Publication 800-207: Zero Trust Architecture. National Institute of Standards and Technology, U.S. Department of Commerce.
  Available at:
  https://nvlpubs.nist.gov/nistpubs/SpecialPublications/NIST.SP.800-207.pdf

Forrester Research.

- Kindervag, John. "The Zero Trust Model." Forrester Research, 2010.
  Available through Forrester Research portals and academic libraries.

Gartner.

- "Hype Cycle for Zero Trust Network Access (ZTNA)." Gartner, Inc.
  Available through Gartner's research portal, typically accessed via professional or academic subscriptions.

Singer, P.W., and Allan Friedman.

- *Cybersecurity and Cyberwar: What Everyone Needs to Know.* Oxford University Press, 2014.
  ISBN: 978-0199918119.

Gilman, Evan, and Doug Barth.

- *Zero Trust Networks: Building Secure Systems in Untrusted Networks.*
  O'Reilly Media, 2017.
  ISBN: 978-1491962190.

Microsoft.

- "Zero Trust Security Framework and Best Practices." Microsoft
  Documentation.
  Available at: https://docs.microsoft.com/en-us/zero-trust/

Cybersecurity and Infrastructure Security Agency (CISA).

- "Zero Trust Maturity Model." Cybersecurity and Infrastructure
  Security Agency, U.S. Department of Homeland Security, 2021.
  Available at: https://www.cisa.gov/zero-trust-maturity-model

Darktrace.

- "Using AI for Threat Detection and Response." Darktrace
  Whitepaper, 2022.
  Available at: https://www.darktrace.com/en/white-papers

SANS Institute.

- SEC401: Security Essentials Bootcamp Style. SANS Institute.
  Available at: https://www.sans.org/cyber-security-
  courses/security-essentials-bootcamp-style/

CrowdStrike.

- "CrowdStrike Falcon: Endpoint Detection and Response."
  CrowdStrike, Inc.
  Available at: https://www.crowdstrike.com/

Cloudflare.

- "Understanding DDoS Attacks and Mitigation Strategies." Cloudflare Learning Center.
  Available at: https://www.cloudflare.com/learning/ddos/what-is-a-ddos-attack/

Splunk.

- "User and Entity Behavior Analytics (UEBA) for Security Operations." Splunk Documentation.
  Available at: https://docs.splunk.com/Documentation/UBA

National Cyber Security Centre (NCSC).

- "Zero Trust Architecture Design Principles." NCSC UK, 2020.
  Available at: https://www.ncsc.gov.uk/

AWS Security Hub.

- "Implementing Zero Trust in AWS Environments." Amazon Web Services (AWS).
  Available at: https://aws.amazon.com/security/

OWASP Foundation.

- "OWASP Top 10: Application Security Risks." Open Web Application Security Project, 2021.
  Available at: https://owasp.org/

IEEE Security & Privacy Magazine.

- Various articles on emerging trends in Zero Trust and AI-based cybersecurity.
  Available through IEEE Xplore: https://ieeexplore.ieee.org/

Epilogue - Embracing the Zero Trust Mindset: A Call to Action

As we reach the conclusion of *Zero Trust Playbook: A Cybersecurity Strategy Inspired by the Soccer Field*, it's time to reflect on the journey we have taken through the evolving landscape of **cybersecurity**. The principles of **Zero Trust** challenge us to reimagine how we approach **digital security**, pushing us beyond the comfort of traditional models to a mindset that demands **constant vigilance, dynamic responses**, and a **commitment to adaptability**. Just as a soccer team requires seamless coordination, discipline, and the ability to pivot during a game, a Zero Trust framework calls for an integrated, holistic approach to securing modern digital environments.

Reflections on the Zero Trust Journey

The **Zero Trust model** is more than a technical strategy; it represents a shift in how we think about **trust** in digital interactions. Where previous models relied on **perimeters, firewalls**, and **implicit trust**, Zero Trust focuses on the **continuous validation** of every user, device, and access request. It is a strategy that is as much about **mindset** and **culture** as it is about **technology**.

In our discussions, we explored how the technical skills—such as **EDR, encryption**, and **IAM**—serve as the building blocks of Zero Trust. We saw how **tactical approaches**, including **penetration testing, honeypots**, and **adaptive access control**, enable organizations to proactively identify vulnerabilities and respond to emerging threats. The importance of **physical security**, through the protection of **data centers, IoT devices**, and **biometric authentication**, reminds us that securing digital assets also means securing the physical infrastructures that support them. Finally, the

psychological aspects of Zero Trust highlight the critical role of **leadership**, **culture**, and **policy-making** in sustaining a security-first mindset.

Lessons from the Soccer Analogy

Throughout this book, the analogy of **soccer** has served as a lens through which to understand Zero Trust. The strategies and tactics that win games on the field also resonate with the strategies that keep networks secure. Just as **players** must adapt to shifting dynamics on the field, **cybersecurity professionals** must adapt to evolving threats and unexpected challenges. A successful soccer team embodies **resilience**, **adaptation**, and **strategic foresight**—qualities that are equally essential for implementing a **Zero Trust Architecture**.

This analogy underscores a fundamental truth: **cybersecurity is a team effort**. Every player, from **IT staff** to **executive leadership**, has a role to play in achieving a secure posture. The Zero Trust model is not a static solution; it is an evolving practice that requires the constant participation and engagement of every individual within an organization.

The Future of Zero Trust

As we look ahead, the role of **Zero Trust** will only become more central in the face of **increasingly sophisticated cyber threats**. The rise of **AI**, **machine learning**, and **cloud computing** will continue to reshape the digital landscape, introducing new challenges that demand innovative solutions. Yet, the core principles of Zero Trust—**never trust, always verify**—will remain a guiding light in navigating these changes.

Organizations that succeed in implementing Zero Trust will not only be better prepared to defend against **cyberattacks** but also foster an environment of **security awareness** and **digital responsibility**. This approach can transform the way we think about **risk management, data protection**, and **user privacy**, creating a safer and more resilient digital world.

A Call to Action

As you finish reading this book, consider how you can apply the principles of Zero Trust in your own **cybersecurity journey**. Whether you are a **student** starting your career, a **practitioner** deepening your expertise, or a **leader** guiding your organization's security strategy, you have the power to make a difference. Zero Trust is not a one-time solution but a continuous process—one that requires your **commitment** to **learning, adapting,** and **leading** with a security-first mindset.

The road to Zero Trust may be challenging, but it is one worth traveling. By embracing its principles and putting them into practice, you will not only enhance the security of your organization but also contribute to the **greater good** of a secure and **trustworthy digital ecosystem.** Let the lessons learned here inspire you to become a **champion of Zero Trust,** just as a great coach inspires their team to reach new heights.

Closing Thoughts

As we close this book, remember that the true power of **Zero Trust** lies in its ability to transform uncertainty into **confidence,** chaos into **control,** and risk into **resilience.** In the ever-changing game of cybersecurity, the best defense is not just a strong perimeter, but a **mindset** that is always ready to **adapt, evolve,** and **protect.**

Thank you for joining me on this journey through the **Zero Trust Playbook.** May the insights, strategies, and lessons within these pages empower you to lead with **confidence, resilience,** and **integrity** as you face the challenges of tomorrow's digital world.

ABOUT THE AUTHOR

Prof. Jerry Yonga is a cybersecurity expert with over **thirty years** of experience in **information technology**, specializing in **Zero Trust Architecture (ZTA)** and **digital transformation**. He has taught **project management** and **cybersecurity** courses at various U.S. universities, mentoring students and guiding them through real-world applications of cybersecurity principles. As a consultant, he helps organizations adopt **Zero Trust models**, focusing on **identity management, cloud security**, and **incident response**. Prof. Yonga has authored numerous books, blending technical depth with engaging storytelling, including *Zero Trust Playbook: A Cybersecurity Strategy Inspired by the Soccer Field*. His work is dedicated to equipping the next generation of cybersecurity leaders with practical insights and strategies.

www.ingramcontent.com/pod-product-compliance
Lightning Source LLC
La Vergne TN
LVHW051640050326
832903LV00022B/830